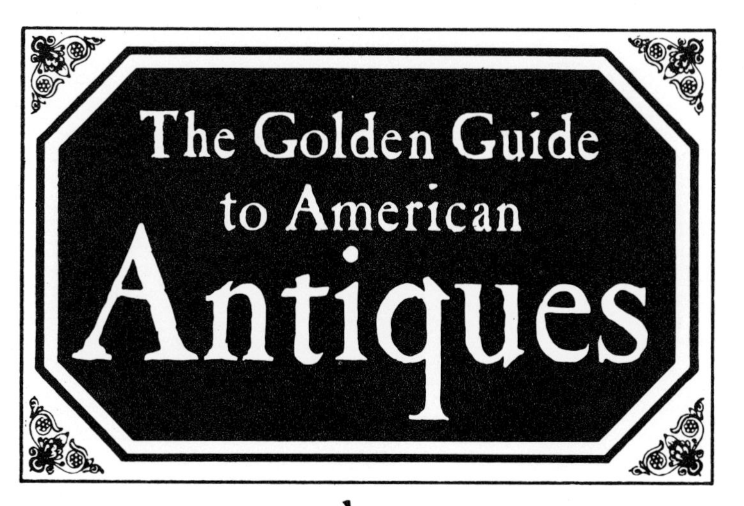

by
Ann Kilborn Cole

Photo Credits

Cover: David Namias (courtesy Red Crow Antiques)

BENNINGTON MUSEUM: 62 top right, 63
CORNING MUSEUM OF GLASS: 64 top left, 70 bottom left & right
HALLMARK GALLERY (Collection of Jerry Smith): 148 left & right
HUDSON SHOP, REDBANK, N.J.: 136 bottom left.
MILDRED & HERBERT KAUFMANN: 23, 35 bottom, 43 nos. 1 & 2
LEES STUDIO: 45 right
MARYLAND HOUSE AND GARDEN PILGRIMAGE (courtesy Mr. & Mrs. John G. Cockey): 15
METROPOLITAN MUSEUM OF ART: 16-17, 21 top & bottom left, 22, 24 top left & right, 26 left, 27, 28 top, bottom right, 35 top, 37 bottom left, 38 nos. 1 & 3, 43 nos. 3 & 4, 44, 54 left, 56 right, 57 left & right, 59 top left, right, 84 top right, 107, 110 bottom, 113 bottom center, 114 bottom right, 122, 123 middle right, 131 center, 135 left & center, 136 top left.
MUSEUM OF THE CITY OF NEW YORK: 31 bottom left
NEW YORK ANTIQUES FAIR: 111, 113 top (by Henry J. Fullerton), 146 top
DAVID NAMIAS: 7, 12, 48. Also (courtesy Lillian Blankley Cogan and Annual Winter Antiques Show, N.Y.) 4, (courtesy Abby Aldrich Rockefeller Folk Art Collection, Williamsburg, Virginia) 118, (courtesy Anton Hardt) 104 middle, (courtesy Baltimore & Ohio Railroad Museum) 146 bottom, (courtesy Katonah, N.Y., Village Library) 128, (courtesy Mildred & Herbert Kaufmann) 52, 150 top.
PARKE BERNET GALLERIES: 24 bottom, 37 bottom right, 98
PHILADELPHIA INQUIRER: 41 left, 54 right, 83 top left (by Dan Weidner), 92 top, 114 top, 131 right, 132 top left, 138 left, 155 bottom
PHILADELPHIA MUSEUM OF ART: 26 right, 32 middle left, 60 no. 1.
VICTORIA & ALBERT MUSEUM: 104 bottom
DAN WEIDNER: 8, 9, 10, 11, 28 bottom left, 31 top left, right, 32 top, middle right, bottom, 37 top right, 38 nos. 2 & 4, 40, 41 right, 43 no. 5, 47, 60 nos. 2, 3, & 4, 62 top left, 64 top right, 65, 66, 69, 70 top, 72, 73, 74, 76, 80 middle left & right, bottom, 83 top right, bottom, 84 top left, bottom, 87 left, 90 top left, 92 bottom, 93, 95, 96 bottom left & right, 99, 100, 103, 104 top, 106, 108, 109, 110 top, 113 bottom right, 114 bottom left, 120, 123 top left, bottom, 125, 127 top left & bottom, 131 left, 132 top right, bottom, 135 top & bottom right, 136 right, 138 right, 139, 150 bottom left & right, 152, 153, 155 top. Also (courtesy Reading Art Museum) 45 left; (courtesy Chester County Historical Society) 96 top, 121; (courtesy Henry Kaufmann) 90 top right; (courtesy Mary Merritt Doll Museum) 140, 142, 143, 144, 149, 156; (courtesy Merritt's Museum of Americana) 87 right, 88 top right, 113 bottom left; (courtesy Robert Merritt) 37 top left, 80 top, 91; (courtesy James G. Pennypacker) 56 left, 59 bottom left, 88 top left, middle, bottom, 116, 117, 123 top right, middle left, 148 top; (courtesy Pennsylvania Farm Museum) 123 center; (courtesy Pottstown Manor) 21 top right; (courtesy Herbert Schiffer) 21 bottom right, 124 left & right, 127 top right; (courtesy Thomas Schock) 67.

 Designed and produced by The Ridge Press, Inc. Printed in the United States of America by Western Printing and Lithographing Company. Published by Golden Press, Inc., New York. Library of Congress Catalog Card Number: 67-10302

Contents

About Collecting

What Is an Antique?

Age is the one quality common to all antiques. American antiques, the subject of this guide, may vary in age from 300 years to 75 or even 50, though the later ones, from the 1860's through 1910, should be called late antiques. The U.S. Customs Service, in deciding import duties, now defines antiques as anything at least 100 years old. Until 1967, imported items could not date from later than 1830 to qualify as antiques. Customs took this date as marking the transition from hand to mechanized manufacture. The new definition takes account of the fact that, as time passes, antiques will be more and more the products of mechanized manufacture.

What, then, gives an old piece the status of an antique? First, it should possess an element of charm, a suggestion of the creative act in its concept, design, or execution.

It may be a work of extraordinary craftsmanship or beauty . . . a simple, functional article that evokes a past way of life . . . the creation of a careful but amateur hand . . . a piece of mechanical ingenuity, a knick-knack of some sort, or a souvenir.

Its charm may lie in being unique; or, on the other hand, in the fact that it can be matched and collected in sets.

The common and contemporary product is never an antique, yet time and increasing rarity can make it one.

Where to Buy Antiques?

Antiques can be found in every locality.

Shops, the primary source, vary greatly in the selectivity of their wares, but they do offer a concentration of antiques, which, in the better shops, have been screened for authenticity and condition.

Shows, a yearly occurrence in most well-populated areas, bring together the best that dealers from near and far have to offer.

Auctions are another source. Many auctioneers have mailing lists and send out notices of upcoming sales. Anything the collector wants to bid for at auction, especially in the higher price ranges, should be examined closely before the sale starts, or even, if necessary, during the bidding.

"Flea markets," where dealers congregate and sell their wares from station wagons, are an increasingly popular weekend phenomenon. Items offered are of the smaller sort, usually with a salting of bargains.

What to do about the hard-to-find antique? Here the lively collectors' grapevine comes into play. If a piece exists at all, it can almost always be turned up in time through inquiries to dealers and advertisements in the antiques magazines.

Geography has little bearing on the antiques trade. The California shop looks much like one in New England, with the addition of some peculiarly western items such as leather pieces and ranch hardware, some Spanish-style things, and imports from the days of the sailing trade with the Orient. Most of the American antiques found in the West are things either brought from the East by early settlers or more lately shipped in by dealers.

Bird's-eye view of large antiques show, with dealers' displays set up in partitioned areas. Wide variety of wares is offered for sale, both buyers and browsers acquire greater knowledge of antiques.

JOHN McCANN

What Collectible to Choose?

The collector's choice is made after first answering certain questions.

"What am I naturally attracted to?" In deciding what to collect, the individual simply acquaints himself with the range of available antiques and then follows the leanings of his taste and pocketbook. There is something for everyone and certainly no excuse for half-hearted collecting.

"What place in my life and home can I give to a collection?" A collection must be suited to the time available and the place where it will be housed. Dolls, for example, need upkeep; furniture needs space; the rarer collectibles take time to find. In a home where there are active children, the collector may enjoy Tôleware more than Tiffany "Favrile."

"How much can I spend?" On a limited antique budget consider souvenir spoons, bells, pressed glass, or one of the dozens of other items that are inexpensive or moderately expensive. If expensive preferences

can be indulged, there are rarities such as cameo glass, early silver, 18th century furniture, and mechanical banks. In antiques, however, the rewards of collecting are not measured by the dollar investment; they are the same whether much is spent or little.

The beginner learns to respect antiques and to accept the fact that it takes years of study and experience to become an expert in any particular field. It's certainly best to "think small" at the outset, since collections can be counted on to change for the better as the collector becomes more knowledgeable and discriminating.

When Is a Piece Worth Buying?

Many a novice collector has come home triumphantly after having paid what an experienced buyer would know to be an outrageous price for either a blatant reproduction or some ordinary piece sold as a "jewel in the rough." Such beginner's mistakes can be avoided. There are specific points on which to judge the worth and desirability of a piece.

Opposite page: An assortment of favored collectibles in glass, china, and metalware. Above: A bad buy. "Married" table has top from early country piece and Empire-style pedestal base.

Pine settee at right was found in condition shown below. It has been well restored, with missing pieces replaced and wood refinished to bring out patina.

First, **authenticity.** This should never be taken for granted, though it may be less of a problem in those categories of items that would be either impossible or unprofitable to reproduce exactly, such as dolls or quilts. In establishing the authenticity of antiques of the kinds that have long been the prey of fakers, like china, brass, furniture, and pressed glass, much depends on the collector's own knowledge and the integrity of the dealer. Now and then the origin of a piece is documented by bills, wills, letters, or inventories. In any case, always examine pieces closely for evidence of the period and the maker from which they are supposed to have come. Marks may be found, especially on china, silver, pewter, some glass, and occasionally furniture. In furniture, every surface, hidden ones especially, should be scrutinized. The more you know, the less danger there is of being taken in by a new thing passed off as old.

Condition should be as near as possible to *proof,* or perfect, although such pieces are at a premium. It is often necessary to settle for cracked, nicked, worn, corroded, or moth-eaten antiques. If the damaged piece is rare and important, it may be worth buying and repairing. And, with pieces intended only for display, the damage may not really matter. Remember, however,

that such pieces never bring top prices at resale, so don't hesitate to pass up something if its liabilities outweigh its assets.

Restored furniture probably has had broken or missing pieces replaced. To remain an antique, such a piece should be at least 60% original. A "married" piece, made up of parts of two or more similar old pieces, is acceptable if you know what you are getting and paying for. A piece newly made of "old wood" is still a reproduction.

Knowing **values and prices** is a sixth sense the collector acquires. There are no rules for judging whether a piece is fairly priced, but guidelines can be found in antiques magazines and price guides. Bargaining is not so much of a factor as people seem to think. Most established dealers quote the price they expect to get for a piece, and stick to it.

Prices for fad collectibles rise quickly, and can slump just as quickly when the fad passes. But with truly fine antiques, value may increase up to 10% per year.

The final decision on a piece involves the collector's own **taste.** The piece that is authentic, well preserved, and reasonably priced is a good buy *only* if it pleases the collector's eye and enhances his collection.

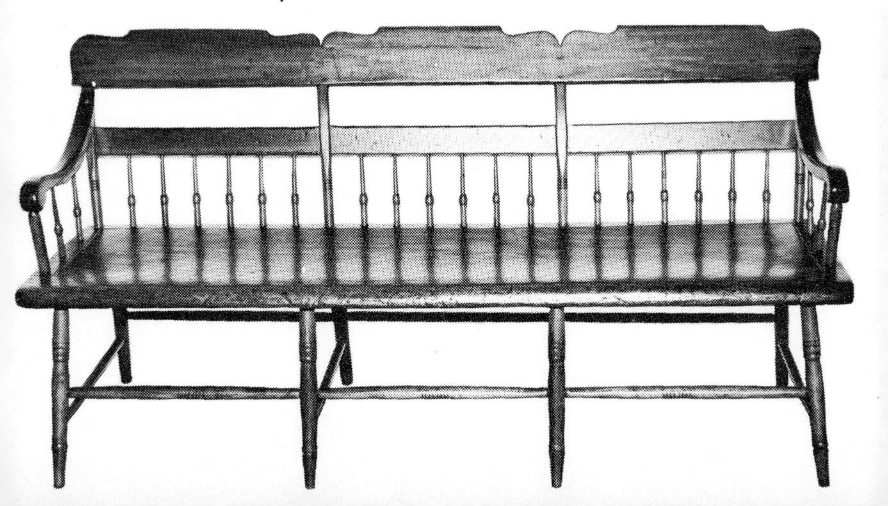

How to Learn About Antiques

A collector must learn to have an "eye" and a "feel" for good, authentic examples in the field of his chosen collectible. To do this he must observe and handle them whenever and wherever possible: in **shops,** at **shows** and **auctions,** in the **homes of other collectors. Museums** are the places to study (if not to handle) the finest examples in every field of antiques, and there are many throughout the country with excellent collections of Americana.

The collector should take advantage of the fact that wherever there are antiques, there are usually professionals who are happy to discuss them. This is particularly so with **historical restorations,** where a broad range of antiques are displayed in their appropriate settings. Thanks to state agencies and historical societies an increasing number of notable colonial and pioneer houses are being preserved and restored to their original condition, complete with furnishings.

Duke of Gloucester Street in Williamsburg, Va., an authentic 18th-century town. Visitors see crafts, costumes, and customs of colonial days.

On the grand scale are the restorations of entire villages, which show how Americans lived hundreds of years ago. In such settings, antiques reveal their full charm and utility. The most extensive restorations are found east of the Mississippi. Among the finest of these are Williamsburg, Va.; Old Sturbridge Village, Mass.; the Farmers' Museum, Cooperstown, N.Y.; Shelburne Village and Museum, Vt.; Old Salem Restoration, Winston-Salem, N.C.; and Henry Ford's Greenfield Village, Dearborn, Mich. West of the Mississippi, there are groups of restored 18th and 19th century buildings in Little Rock, Ark.; San Antonio, Tex.; Monterey, Calif.; and Virginia City, Nev. New Orleans, La., has some well preserved 17th and 18th century buildings.

First-hand experience should be reinforced by **reading.** There are books on every subject of interest to antiques collectors. Whatever is required, whether it be a history of silverware, a dictionary of china marks, or a guide to restoring furniture, there is expert guidance and comprehensive information available. There are also several magazines devoted to antiques in general, such as **Spinning Wheel, Antiques, Hobbies,** and **The Antiques Journal.** Magazines for women, notably **Woman's Day,** frequently have excellent articles on antiques. Community libraries are still the best places to start the search for information. They are able to refer the reader to the sources of any reading matter not actually on their shelves. And what they do have in books and back numbers of magazines is valuable, whatever the date of publication.

Of all the ways of learning about antiques, **membership in an antiques club or society** is perhaps the most enjoyable. There are, for example, national organizations for collectors of specialties such as buttons, dolls, music boxes, paperweights, pewter, playing cards, watches, and guns. "The Questers," a society for collectors of antiques of all kinds, has more than a hundred chapters scattered across the country. Many communities have clubs that keep members well informed through guest speakers, study projects, field trips, and periodical bulletins. To know what organizations exist and what they are doing, read the antiques magazines.

How to Display a Collection

Showing off a collection is almost as important as acquiring it. Even the most valuable collection loses interest when it is not kept clean, bright, and presentable.

Many people like to work their antique pieces into their home décor. Usually one good cabinet can hold an entire collection and becomes an additional attraction if it is an antique itself, such as a corner cupboard or a Victorian what-not cabinet. Window shelves display glass to advantage and take up little space. Many things, like old valentines, fans, and buttons, can be framed and hung like pictures.

How to Protect a Collection

Beyond usual safekeeping, good antiques should be insured against theft, breakage, and vandalism. This is done by taking out a Fine Arts policy, either separately or as part of comprehensive household coverage. Anything that qualifies as an antique can be insured, from a wrought-iron weathervane to a Hepplewhite sideboard. Pieces must be itemized and a value assigned to each. The owner's evaluation of the pieces listed is usually accepted by the insurer; however, very valuable pieces may require a professional appraisal. Premiums are quite reasonable. A typical premium might be $75 for a declared valuation of $5,000. If prices or items in the collection change, it is a simple matter to revise the figures and the premium.

A rising market and regional differences in prices make close dollar valuations of collectible antiques impractical. Instead, a price range is indicated, using asterisks as symbols, that will give the reader an idea of the cost of collecting in any given category. Prices are for representative pieces in average good condition.

* *(Inexpensive) $1 to $25*
** *(Moderately Expensive) $25 to $100*
*** *(Expensive) $100 to $500*
**** *(Very Expensive) $500 and up*

Early American room shows charming use of antiques for home décor.

Furniture

The essential fact about a piece of antique furniture is that its charm and value are not diminished by time. Furthermore, antiques can often be had for not much more than the cost of new furniture, sometimes even for less. Little wonder, then, that so many people choose to furnish their homes with antiques.

The beginner should go slow in buying antique furniture. The wisest procedure is to visit many shops, talk to the dealers, and survey the many items and styles available. If truly fine antiques are the collector's dream, and funds are low, he can make one such acquisition a year or at even longer intervals. This is better than rushing in to buy inferior pieces. Once a purchase is decided on, it should be made through a trustworthy and knowledgeable dealer.

Even the first piece should fit into a scheme for present or future décor. Pieces from different style periods can be mixed, but if the charm of antiques is to have its full effect, a certain unity of feeling should be observed, either of elegance or simplicity, of formality or comfort.

Country furniture, or Early American, as decorators call it, is often the choice of beginning collectors. It includes two large categories of antiques: furniture items made in the simplest, most functional manner to do duty in country and farm homes, and those made in the general lines of established styles, but without the refinement of pieces originally intended for elegantly appointed town or manor houses. It's possible, for example, to buy a very pleasing country chest in Sheraton style for far less than a Sheraton chest of mahogany done by a very sophisticated cabinetmaker. Yet both can be found in the rich treasury of American antique furniture.

Preceding pages: Room in American wing, Metropolitan Museum of Art, New York City. Furniture pieces are among finest ever made in United States.

A thumbnail sketch of the history of antique furniture in America begins with the Puritan era, whose massive and angular furniture survives today mostly in museums and restorations. Succeeding styles emanated from England, largely by way of pattern books published by the designers Chippendale, Hepplewhite, and Sheraton. These styles were interpreted by American craftsmen, whose individuality of skill and imagination produced a range of furniture that runs from country pieces of unadorned pine to the superb Philadelphia-made mahogany highboys that today command prices in the tens of thousands of dollars.

Early Empire, exemplified in the well-known work of New York cabinetmaker Duncan Phyfe, was the last of the major style periods before the mass production of furniture began in the 1830's. For almost a century thereafter, until the advent of Modern in the 1920's, furniture designers, a few rebels excepted, disdained lightness and simplicity. With the opening of the Victorian era, in the 1840's, furniture turned to plush upholstery and generous curves. By 1875 it had grown to monumental proportions—the logical expression, perhaps, of the expansionist mentality of the times.

An historical factor affecting the evolution of American furniture was the westward advance of the frontier. Styles took decades to spread westward and usually arrived long after the fashions in the East had changed. This created what is called survival furniture, pieces made in styles that had already been superseded.

Confronted with so many styles and variations, it is up to the buyer to judge for himself the many points that add up to quality and worth in a piece—materials, finish, workmanship, and grace of shape and proportion. So before he buys, he should educate his eye.

Early Style Periods

WILLIAM AND MARY (****) c. 1700–25, was the final, graceful stage of the long period during which English furniture was characterized by dark woods and a look of angular solidity. Some characteristics of this style are trumpet-shaped or spiral legs, serpentine stretchers crossed diagonally between the legs, ball feet, use of burled veneer, and teardrop-handled drawer pulls. Some chair backs had a slight inward curve to fit the body. Preferred wood was walnut. In this style look for stretcher and gate-leg tables, ball-foot chests. Rare.
QUEEN ANNE (***/****) c. 1720–50, imposed curves upon a basically angular structure. The style is known, above all, for the cabriole leg, later carried on with embellishments by Chippendale. The Dutch or pad foot is the most frequent termination of the cabriole leg. Except for the carved shell or fan decoration, surface interest depends on wood grain and use of veneer, giving an all-over effect of simplicity compared with earlier styles. Tables and frame pieces often have scrolled aprons. Chairs have vertical splat backs. Walnut and mahogany are the preferred woods; country versions are also found in cherry and maple. Key plates and mounts of drawer pulls are batwing in shape. Look for chairs, lowboys and highboys, card, tea, and drop-leaf tables. Available.

Pricing for antique furniture presents special problems: (1) the importance of the piece in relation to other forms in its style; and (2) the degree of refinement in the execution of a piece.

For instance, a Chippendale chair would cost less than a Chippendale highboy, and a country version of a Chippendale chest would cost less than a finely-made piece. Symbols do not refer to the generally lower prices of country versions; rather, they refer to pieces that are truly representative of the style and apply to the articles that are mentioned as most readily available.

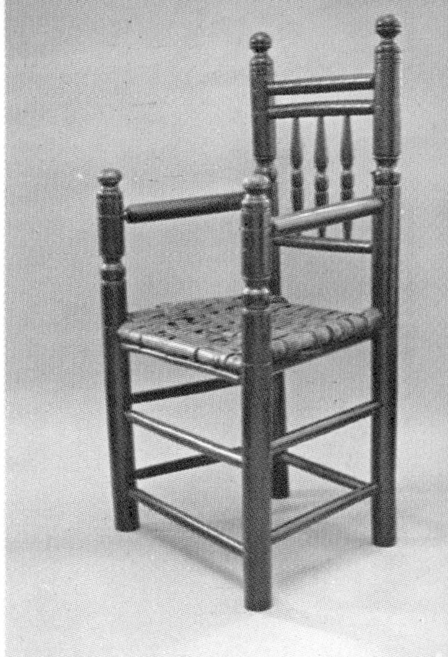

Top left: William & Mary table has trumpet-turned legs with serpentine stretchers. Top right: Governor Carver chair of Puritan period. Bottom: Queen Anne chair and highboy with characteristic cabriole legs, batwing handles, shell carving.

CHIPPENDALE (***/****) c. 1750–90, was first described by its creator, Thomas Chippendale, in his *Gentlemen and Cabinet Maker's Directory,* published in 1754. It developed into a richly masculine style, incorporating elements of Gothic, rococo, and Chinese design, and, in later pieces, the classic principles of the brothers Adam, designers of architectural details and appointments for the fine houses of England.

Chippendale produced a full range of home furnishings, including desks and chests with bow and serpentine fronts, tilt-top tables with piecrust edging, settees, and chairs. Chippendale chair legs have a short, wide set; in style, they are either cabriole–often with rococo carving at the knee–or square, in the Chinese manner. The backs of the chairs have a shouldered look due to the up-tilting of the ends of the top rail. Chests stand usually on ogee-molded bracket feet.

American furniture makers elaborated freely on the basic elements of Chippendale design. The ball and claw foot was incorporated; Philadelphia cabinetmakers Benjamin Randolph and William Savery made highboys of superb proportion, with intricate carving and scrolled tops; New England wedded Chippendale to the block-front design at which its makers excelled, especially Goddard and Townsend of Newport, R.I.

Mahogany was the preferred wood for Chippendale, though walnut, maple, and cherry also were much used. Decorative motifs include scrolls, finials, carved shells, and acanthus leaves; Chinese-style pieces feature fret-work. The brass mounts of drawer pulls on American pieces are ornate and intricately curved. In Chippendale style look for side chairs, piecrust tables, Pembroke tables, chests, mirrors, desks, secretaries, lowboys, settees. Available.

Left: Chippendale chair in modified Chinese style has sturdy proportions, shouldered top rail. Center: Tilt-top table has piecrust edging, pedestal base with claw-footed cabriole legs. Above: Transitional country chest with bracket feet.

HEPPLEWHITE (***/****) c. 1785–1800, was a revelation to American cabinetmakers when trade between England and America resumed after the Revolution. The lightly graceful, classic style was nothing like the Chippendale it succeeded. As set down by George Hepplewhite in his *Cabinet Maker's and Upholsterer's Guide,* published in 1788, it called for straight, slim, tapering legs, with the body of the piece in correspondingly light proportions. Decoration was subtle, achieved by the use of graining, inlaid motifs, and shallow carving. Splayed French feet were used on chests. The sideboard made its first appearance, often with a gracefully curved or serpentine front. Tambour doors gave elegance to desks and sewing tables. Hepplewhite chairs featured backsplats in endless variations of the sheaf motif. Plain chairs had humpback top rails and square, stretcher-braced legs. Fancier chairs had tapering, unbraced legs and often the familiar shield back. Also characteristic of this style are the oval-shaped brass mounts of the drawer pulls. Preferred wood was mahogany, and—for popular light-toned pieces—satinwood. The finest American Hepplewhite, exquisitely inlaid, was made in Baltimore.

In this style look for sideboards, card tables, sewing tables, side chairs, desks, Pembroke tables. Available.

Top left: Pembroke table in Hepplewhite style has shallow leaves, tapering legs, center drawer with oval handle. Top right: Shield-back arm chair with characteristic "camel back" top rail and flared rectangular seat; striped covering for seat is frequent, as is use of brass-headed tacks for decoration. Bottom: Sideboard, an innovation of this period, has delicate fruitwood inlay, with bellflower motif on tapering legs.

SHERATON (**/****) c. 1795–1820, closely followed Hepplewhite, and much American furniture made during its period of vogue is a blending of the two styles. But furniture that closely followed the designs in Thomas Sheraton's pattern book, *The Cabinet-Maker and Upholsterer's Drawing Book*, published in parts between 1791 and 1794, is highly distinctive. The rectangle is basic to this style, with the vertical lines (legs, corners of case pieces, etc.) often reeded and fluted for interest. Legs usually are turned and tapered. Chair backs are especially rectangular in feeling; the splatting, however, is very delicately shaped, with members often turned or curved in elegant motifs.

Many Sheraton chests have fluted columns at the corners and stand on spindly legs. Pedestal bases of three and four legs are frequent on late Sheraton tables.

Left: Sheraton work table has strong rectangular feeling, turned, tapered legs, rosette drawer pulls. Center: Similar features are seen in colonnette-back arm chair. Right: Pair of Directoire saber-leg chairs.

Rosette, lion head, and hexagonal oblong mounts were used for drawer pulls.

Mahogany was the choice wood, often with contrasting inlay of satinwood. In the Sheraton styles look for sofas, side chairs, beds, sideboards, sewing tables, chests of drawers. Available.

AMERICAN DIRECTOIRE (**/***) c. 1805–15, was inspired by the graceful, classical-motif furniture of the French Directoire and was made with great distinction by Duncan Phyfe. The style retains the strong horizontals of Sheraton design, but in most cases boldly curved lines are also integral. The lyre shape is seen in chair backs, table bases, and the side arms of sofas, while "saber" legs and curule bases (see p. 36) are the usual supports; decoration is restrained. Pieces are occasionally available, often designated "Late Federal."

EMPIRE furniture (**/***) c. 1810–40, emerged during the Napoleonic era and, indeed, there is something of an air of triumph about it, even in its American versions. Thomas Sheraton became one of its chief exponents with his designs after 1810, known as "Late Sheraton," while Duncan Phyfe became perhaps the best-known worker in the new style. Like Directoire, it emphasized classical motifs, but its overall design was far more heavily proportioned. Busily-carved friezes and pilasters accentuated basic lines. Ogee columns flanked the drawers of chests, which often had overhanging top drawers. Constantly recurring forms were the 3- or 4-foot pedestal base in table supports and the lyre shape both in supporting members and in chair backs. Also characteristic were claw feet and brackets carved to look like winged creatures. The eagle became a favorite motif for inlay, while leaves, grain, fruit, and other carvings spread bounteously over legs, arms, and other appropriate surfaces. This was the furniture of the American Greek Revival period, c. 1810–30, when almost every new building had a columned porch.

"Late Empire" (1825–50) comprises the utterly graceless forms to which the fashion gradually tended, until being displaced by Victorian at about midcentury.

Mahogany, cherry, and maple were the preferred woods for Empire furniture, often with a reddish stain.

In Empire style, look for sleigh beds, lyre-base side tables, sofas with rolled top rails, chests, pier tables, "classic" chairs. Available.

Top: Sofa, attributed to Phyfe, has lyre-shaped side arms, claw feet with cornucopia brackets. Far left: Simple Empire bureau with side pillars, overhanging drawer. Left: Card table has lyre-motif pedestal, leaf carving on legs.

Victorian

Victorian furniture, c. 1840–1900, covers the styles that developed during Queen Victoria's long reign. Almost all of them were inspired by earlier designs and were marked by exaggerated ornamentation. The interest of the collector is in those forms which, heavy as they are, have a certain grace and the charm of Victorian coziness.

EARLY VICTORIAN (**/***) c. 1840–55, is fairly pleasing and unpretentious, especially the pieces whose curves harken back to Early Empire. General features are bracket feet, wavy molding, applied carving, and imaginative use of veneer. Preferred woods were walnut, rosewood, and mahogany, and in country furniture maple and butternut. In Early Victorian, look for arm and side chairs and settees. Available.

VICTORIAN GOTHIC (**/***) c. 1840–65, is small and light, in contrast to the bulky medieval furniture it pretends to imitate. Its Gothic-inspired ornamentation features intricate tracery, pointed arches on chairs and chests, elongated chair backs. Preferred woods were walnut, mahogany, rosewood. In this style, look for chairs, beds, cabinets. Available.

COTTAGE furniture (**) c. 1840–60 was the first low-cost, mass-produced furniture, and it made the charming furniture of the country artisans a thing of the past. It was Victorian, styled for the new rural middle class. Painted or mahogany stained, it was smallish in proportion and fairly lightweight, being made of soft woods. Bedroom pieces, especially mirrored chests with two drawers set apart at either side of the top, are the most common relics of this style. Readily available.

VICTORIAN LOUIS XV furniture (**/***) c. 1845–70, also called **Victorian rococo,** was a revival of an or-

Above left: Early Victorian side chair with bold carving, curves in back, legs, seat. Left: In typical Victorian Gothic chair, straight back has quatrefoil tracery, pointed arch and side rails. Above: Painted "cottage" chest with attached mirror, marble top.

Four expressions of Victorian taste. Reading clockwise: Spool-turned table; Eastlake side chair; medallion-back sofa remarkable for well-executed carving on frame; prize Belter chair in rococo style.

nate 18th-century style in which the cabriole leg was a basic element. The scrolled and serpentine contours in fashion during the reign of Louis XV were exaggerated in the Victorian version, the ornate carving of shells, fruits, flowers, and birds made bolder and more florid. The best and most prized American furniture in this style was the sumptuous work of John Henry Belter, made in New York City c. 1840–60. Belter developed a process for laminating wood so that it could be bent and carved in unusually intricate designs. He worked in the stylish woods, especially rosewood and mahogany. In Victorian rococo, look for parlor sets of chairs for a lady and gentleman—the latter with arms, sofas, slipper chairs, and marble-topped tables.

SPOOL-TURNED furniture (**) c. 1850–70, was machine-lathed so that posts, rails, legs, and spindles simulate a succession of spool, knob, button, sausage, base-and-ring, or ball-and-disk shapes. It was mass-produced, mostly in the cheaper woods (maple, cherry, birch), and was usually stained or painted. Occasional mahogany productions were simply varnished.

Favorites in this style are Jenny Lind beds, with low headboards, named for the famous Swedish singer who toured the U.S. between 1850–52. Available.

EASTLAKE furniture (**) c. 1870–90, was inspired by the book *Hints on Household Taste*, written by the English architect Charles L. Eastlake and published here in 1872. Rectilinear in form, it was ornamented with shallow carving, framed paneling, false drawer fronts, and oxidized or brass-plated hardware. Oak and other light-toned woods were preferred. Though certainly not beautiful, it was inexpensive and widely admired. Today an Eastlake chair or washstand may be picked up to fill out a Victorian setting. Available.

Special Chairs

WINDSOR CHAIRS (**/***) are said to have originated in the 17th century near Windsor Castle, southwest of London. Basically, a Windsor is constructed of a thick saddle seat into which spindles are set at carefully calculated angles to form a curved, slanting back. Top ends of the spindles are anchored in a rail that may be either straight, as in the comb-back Windsor, or in an inverted U-shape, as in bow-back Windsors. H-shape stretchers brace the legs.

Around 1725 America enthusiastically adopted this comfortable, lightweight chair, first in Philadelphia and soon after—with many regional variations—throughout New England and New Jersey. The two major schools of design which resulted were the Philadelphia Windsor, often with ball feet, and the more delicate New England. By 1800, Windsor construction was so popular in America that its style was adapted for high chairs, settees, and rockers. The woods preferred in early Windsors were hickory, ash, and oak—often in combination, and the chairs usually were painted. As the chair became common, soft woods and mahogany were used. In judging a Windsor, look for hardwood construction, a bold rake to the legs, a generous number of spindles (nine preferred), a gracefully molded seat, and a general lightness of feeling. Familiar forms and variations include: side chairs, arm chairs, writing arm chairs (rare), bow-, comb-, fan-, and brace-back Windsors (the last with two or four extra spindles set into a rear extension of the seat), the Boston rocker, and the sturdy, low-back captain's chair. Available.

FANCY CHAIRS, a vogue between 1810 and 1860, were just what the name implies. Whatever the level of a room's sophistication, a fancy chair was meant to add a dash of beauty and spice.

Left: Comb-back Windsor is fine example of form. Spindles are angled in gently curving back, thick plank seat is cut from single piece of wood; arm through which spindles pass is also of one piece. Note rake of legs and bulbous, H-shaped stretcher. Above: Pennsylvania Windsor settee has many points in common with familiar "captain's chair," including low back and continuation of spindles to front of seat.

Sheraton fancy chairs, fashioned of mahogany, were light in appearance and usually had rush or cane seats. Carving, painting, gilding, and stenciling were the modes of decoration. The same treatment was also applied to chairs of Hepplewhite design. Such chairs are rare and expensive (***).

Hitchcock chairs (**) of the antique period, c. 1810–60, are small light chairs with rolled top rails and rush seats. The frame was usually painted black and decorated with gold stenciling. They are available but hard to authenticate, as reproductions abound.

Pennsylvania plank seat chairs (**) were often painted with bright colors to make them "fancy." Available.

CLASSIC CHAIRS (**/***) incorporating forms from Greek, Roman, and Egyptian antiquity, include the:

klismos, recognized by its saber legs, the front and rear sets curving away from each other;

curule, with legs formed by crossed cyma curves— ;

Egyptian, basically of the klismos type, but with the addition of motifs such as leaves, wings, and claws.

FAVORITE COLLECTORS' ITEMS

Carpet Cutter Rocker: Has very thin rocker blades.

Lincoln Rocker: Upholstered chair of the 1860–75 period, has low seat, high back, gracefully curved wood frame.

Mammy Rocker: Settee rocker with one end railed off for a cradle.

Martha Washington: Upholstered, open-arm chair.

Roundabout or Corner Chair: Seat constructed on the diagonal so that sitter's legs straddle corner and supporting leg. Low, open back.

Salem Rocker: Armless version of Boston rocker.

Settee: Seat for two or more persons, with back, arms, and slim legs. Early settees were cane-seated; Chippendale were upholstered; country styles had plank seats and spindle backs.

Slipper Chair: Chair in any style with low seat (for ease in putting on footwear).

Wing Chair: Upholstered piece with high back and wing-like extensions at sides for protection against drafts.

Hitchcock chair

Lincoln rocker

Martha Washington chair

Wing chair

1
2
3
4

Mirrors

Three early mirrors deserve special mention because of their popularity with today's collectors. The **courting mirror** (***) is a small (15 inches high) vanity glass, supposedly brought from China about 1800, although many suggest Dutch origin. Frames are embellished with glass laid into the wood, either as strips painted with flowers, etc., or as bits of colored glass. Many of these mirrors, and the most prized, are found in their original boxes. These mirrors are moderately available. The **shaving mirror** (**), which can be tilted backward or forward, is mounted in a frame attached to a stand. One or two small drawers are sometimes included and the whole piece is designed to sit on top of a bureau or chest (see picture page 23). Also available. **Over-mantel mirrors** (**), oblong in shape, serve best over a mantel, as the name suggests. Available.

Between 1790 and 1810 oval frames were popular, and the round **convex mirror** (***) is a prize piece from this period. The convex shape of the glass brings an entire room into the field of reflection. The round, gilded frames often have eagle finials and are sometimes equipped with candle brackets (girandoles).

Wall mirrors follow the furniture styles of their periods. Queen Anne mirrors (now rare) are long and narrow with carved, crested tops, and sometimes scrolled pediments. Chippendales are elaborate, their frames handsomely carved, many with phoenix finials, and swags or gilt draperies at the sides. Classical motifs are used in the Hepplewhite pieces; the finials become urns filled with delicate gold flowers or sheaves of wheat. The simpler Sheraton mirrors have flat tops, are often ornamented with turned or twisted side pillars, and sometimes by a painted panel above the glass. Victorian frames are ornate, usually of gilded plaster on wood.

1. Courting mirror has colored glass set into frame. 2. Typical convex mirror has eagle pediment and swags. 3 & 4. Sheraton mirrors in formal and country versions share rosette corners, rectangular shape.

Miscellany

The fascination of an antique shop is its rich variety. Here are some unusual furniture items to look for.

ACCESSORIES

Lap or traveling desks, small cases opening up as slanted surface for letter writing. Made in better woods.
Blanket or dower chests, sturdy pine pieces; low ones can do double duty as window seats.
Mule chests, with lift-top, and two or more fake drawers.

CONVERTED PIECES

Spice cabinets, fine for storing small items.
Apothecary cabinets, with many small drawers; ideal as room dividers and for holding small things.
Dry sinks, once kitchen pieces for dish washing; now, lined with copper, hold bar items or indoor plants.
Pie cupboards, with pierced tin panels for ventilation, once used for storing fresh food, now have many uses.
School masters' desks, on tall legs, usually have slanted lid covering storage area.

ARCHITECTURAL PIECES

Corner cupboards, in every style and wood.

Fireplace mantels, lovely ones rescued from old homes.

RURAL FURNITURE

Sawbuck and trestle tables, heavy duty tables for informal rooms.

Harvest tables, long, narrow, drop-leaf tables, capable of seating many hands at harvest time, now useful for buffet entertaining.

Wagon seats, once used in farm wagons, now upholstered, make informal settees for two.

BEDS

Tester beds, tall poster beds with frame for canopy.

Rope beds, with pegged or pierced frames, have woven rope as mattress support.

Trundle beds, small beds, low enough to roll under a large one; usually for children.

Day beds, with matching head and foot boards.

Left: Pennsylvania dry sink, here used for display. Above: Lady's writing box of mid-1800's. Right: Pie safe with punched panels for air circulation.

Regional Furniture

Travelers on the antiques trail will find that many furniture items are strongly associated with certain regions of the United States.

New England is abundant in colonial pine furniture. Favorite pieces are open pewter cupboards, blanket chests, sea chests, ladderback chairs, drop-leaf tables; (*/***).

Seaport towns that prospered from whaling and fishing have furniture of more sophisticated make, from the Queen Anne period through Early Empire.

Two outstanding New England specialties are the butterfly table (rare) with widely flared supporting brackets, and the oak Hadley chest (very rare) with one or two drawers and the front surface heavily carved.

Hudson River Valley was settled by the Dutch, and its furniture has the characteristics of the William and Mary style. Outstanding pieces are heavy chests with ball feet, trestle tables, chests and desks on frames, and the massive *kas*, a two-door wardrobe with overhanging cornice; (***).

Southern furniture of fine quality stood in plantation houses and in the fine town houses of the large Southern cities. Baltimore, Richmond, Savannah, Charleston, and New Orleans all made and used versions of period styles so distinctive that they are often referred to by the name of the city. In New Orleans, the French influence was uppermost.

Two items are peculiar to the South: the sugar chest (for locking away that precious commodity); and the hunt board, a tall, plain sideboard, Hepplewhite in feeling, used for stand-up eating after a hunt (***). Both are occasionally available.

1. New England pewter cupboard with characteristic wrought iron hinges and pivoting latch. 2. New England tea table with button feet. 3. Rare butterfly table. 4. Hudson River kas, *trompe l'oeil decoration. 5. Southern hunt table, Hepplewhite in feeling.*

1

2

3

4

5

Pennsylvania Dutch The folk traditions of the Swiss and Germans who settled the counties northwest of Philadelphia (Lehigh, Lancaster, Lebanon, and Berks) are seen in their highly distinctive furniture, made between the early 1700's and the mid-1800's. Extravagantly colored folk designs—tulips, hearts, distelfinks (small, parrot-like birds), etc.—are often painted against mottled and contrasted backgrounds. These strongly-built pieces, mostly of pine and walnut, include arm chairs, dower chests, hanging wall cupboards, *shranks* (wardrobes), bureaus, dry sinks, dough tables, and Moravian farm tables with detachable tops; (**/***).

Left: Walnut Pennsylvania cupboard has dentil molding around top, scrolled mounts on drawer handles. Below: Pennsylvania Dutch chest. Right: Shaker chair, stand.

Shaker furniture is best found near early settlements of this religious sect in Maine, Massachusetts, Connecticut, New York, Ohio, and Kentucky. Meticulous Shaker craftsmen used conventional colonial forms but stripped them of all worldly embellishments and produced a furniture extraordinary for its lightness and economy of design. Maple, pine, cherry, butternut, walnut, and birch were used, with a special fondness for light-toned woods. Items include ladderback chairs and rockers, candle stands, tables for various uses, cupboards, low-post beds, bureau-desks; (***). Available.

Western furniture In the Southwest: Mexican and Spanish inspired pieces, such as painted Chihuahua chests, trasteros (cupboards with grillwork doors), chip-carved chairs, trestle tables; (***). On the West Coast: more Spanish inspired furniture, plus Oriental items brought in by the China trade, including tables, chests, and sideboards; (***). Moderately available.

Late Antiques

Furniture styles of the last hundred years have not been marked by the lasting character of 18th and early 19th century designs. The public learned to mix styles—almost always with a touch of the exotic, while makers experimented with new materials and techniques. Catalogues of the late Victorian and Edwardian eras offer showy bedroom sets of bird's-eye maple and circassian walnut, pseudo-French parlor pieces, country house suites of wicker and bamboo, iron and brass furniture. Efforts at simplicity produced the crude, slatted "mission" furniture of 1900–10 vogue, and the severely linear furniture of the "crafts" movement in England.

One style, bentwood, has kept its charm. It was developed around 1850 by the Thonets of Vienna, who learned to bend wood into sinuous curves and made furniture in which these curves served functionally. Much came into the U.S., and pieces are available.

The Art Nouveau movement also extended to furniture, though not on a mass-produced basis. Occasionally a piece may be found in the naturalistic, free-flowing lines of this Edwardian-period style.

Ever since decorators discovered the "late antiques" —**bentwood, wicker, brass,** real and imitation **bamboo**— reproductions have multiplied. The collector must look for pieces that will survive the fad, that is, authentic, tasteful originals (**/***).

A group of late antiques enjoying renewed popularity. From top: Thonet bentwood lady's recliner of 1860 prefigured sinuous curves of Art Nouveau; turn-of-the-century brass bed; porch chair in wicker; small stand of mottled bamboo.

Authenticity

Fantastic deceptions are possible in the reproduction of antique furniture. In judging the authenticity of a piece, the beginner has little choice but to rely on the advice of the dealer. The inexperienced buyer

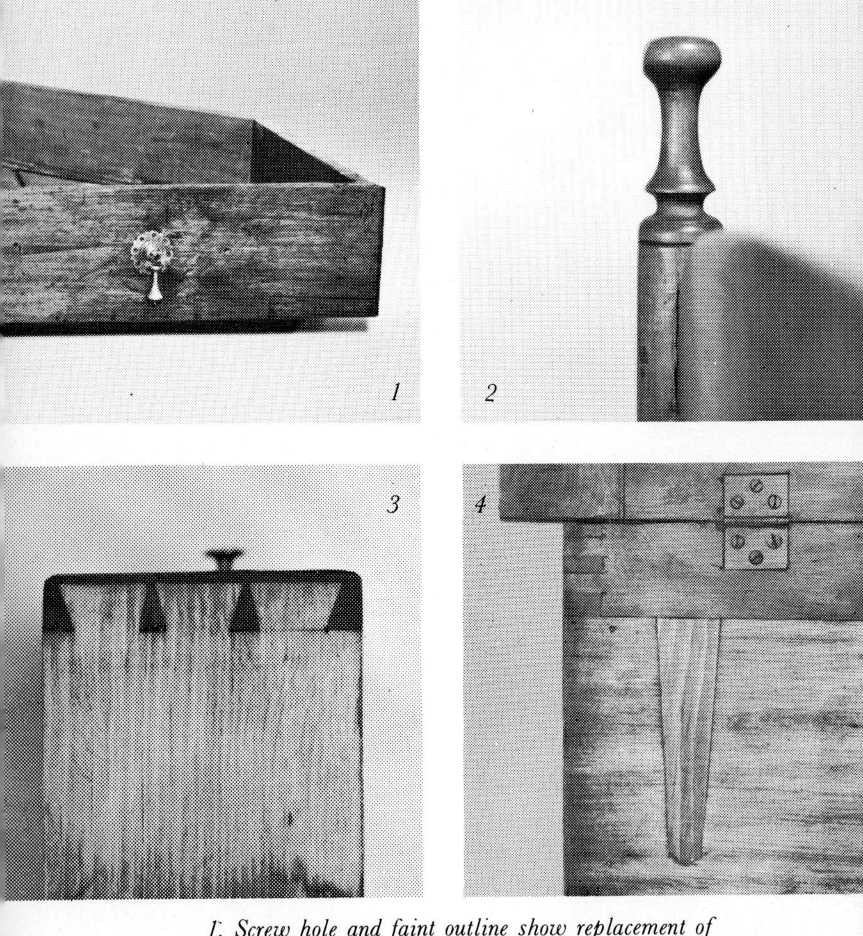

1. Screw hole and faint outline show replacement of batwing drawer pull with teardrop type. 2. Finial is worn from rubbing against wall. 3. Irregular dovetails indicate handwork. 4. Machine sanding and plywood repair have not enhanced old cherry desk.

should become as familiar as possible with the various furniture styles and periods, so that he will be able to talk intelligently with the dealer.

Whether beginner or expert, the buyer should look a piece over very carefully. He should note the replacement of old wood with new, any repairs that have been made and whether they have been done well. He should check for signs of wear (normal or obviously faked), shrinkage (hard to fake), and weakness or rot at points of stress. Since the undersides, backs, and interiors of old American pieces were left raw, furniture with stain, shellac, or varnish on these surfaces always warrants further attention to establish its true background.

Methods of construction tell much. How wood was cut and joined, the hardware used (nails, screws, hinges, etc.), are important signs of authenticity for the various periods. Pieces that still have their original brass drawer pulls and mounts are more valuable for that fact.

CARE OF FURNITURE

Ill usage, not age, is the worst enemy of fine furniture. Joints and dowels loosen when chairs are tipped back by sitters, hinge screws pull out when desk lids are dropped carelessly. Finishes may be seriously marred when hot or abrasive things are placed on them, while strong sunlight beating on a piece can eventually cause its finish to fade and check.

An excessively dry atmosphere causes shrinkage, brittleness, loosening of joints. Owners should keep their central heating systems at moderate temperature and even use humidifiers to keep moisture in the air.

Regular maintenance calls for cleaning, polishing, and repair as needed. It is especially wise to bring children up to treat fine furniture with the care it deserves.

GLOSSARY OF FURNITURE TERMS

Balloon Back: On chairs, wide back splat shaped like a partly inflated balloon. **Fiddle-back,** violin-shaped splat.

Banister Back: A side chair, designed with a crest rail and several split banisters (round spindles), resting on a cross-piece above the seat rail.

Birdcage Table: Tilt-top table with small, square, spindled gallery at top of pedestal base.

Bombé: Furniture style with front and sides swollen, like a kettle.

Bracket Foot: A right-angle support at the corners of a case piece.

Breadboard Ends: The ends of planks on tables, etc. which have been covered with wooden strips to hide raw edges and prevent warping.

Breakfront: A case piece where center portion of front is recessed or projecting.

Bun Foot: Flattened ball foot.

Burl: Beautifully grained wood cut from growths found on tree trunks.

Butler's Desk: Chest of drawers with fall-front top drawer and pigeonhole compartments.

Case Pieces: Furniture basically box-like in structure, including desks, cupboards, chests of drawers, bookcases.

Chamfered: Having a beveled edge.

Chest-on-chest: Case piece of tiered drawers, made in two sections, often with elaborate cornice.

Dentil: a form of decorative molding, notched or serrated.

Dishtop: Table top with raised edge; **piecrust:** when edge is crimped.

Federal Period: Term used for American furniture made in period 1789–1830; includes Hepplewhite, Sheraton, and Empire styles.

Governor Winthrop Desk: A common but erroneous

name for a fallfront, slant-lid desk with drawers.
Ladder Back: Chair style with horizontal splats.
Ogee: A form of molding with a single or double curve.
Ogee Foot: Contoured bracket foot with cyma curves.
Pad, Dutch, Drake, Snake, Club, or Slipper Foot: All terms for flat foot on Queen Anne style cabriole legs.
Patina: In furniture, mellow surface quality that results from age, use, polishing, exposure.
Pembroke Table: Small, elegant, drop-leaf table with tapered legs, used as tea or breakfast table.
Pier Table: Decorative side table usually placed between windows and under a mirror.
Pilaster: Architectural feature used in furniture, with a column and a base.
Plank Seat: Seat made from one piece of wood.
Rabbit-Eared: Term describing chair where end posts of back extend an inch or so beyond the top rail.
Reeding: Parallel, rounded grooving, used on legs and posts.
Rococo: Elaborate relief decoration of French origin which combines shells, rocks, leaves.
Settle: An early wooden bench with tall back and sides, sometimes hooded.
Slip Seat: A chair seat, usually upholstered, removable from the frame.
Splat: Flat, sometimes shaped support in chair backs.
Splay or Rake: The angle of inclination from the perpendicular on chair legs, etc.
Stretcher: Horizontal braces connecting the legs of table or chair.
Tambour: Flexible panel of wood slats glued to canvas.
Tavern Table: Table with a long, broad top and turned legs braced by stretchers placed just above the feet.
Turned: A rounded leg, post, or spindle.

Glass

Glass is deservedly one of the most popular categories of American antiques. There is a marvelous variety of collectibles at every price, and a still greater choice as to styles, patterns, and makers. On display, glass is particularly handsome, yet requires relatively little space.

The history of glassmaking dates back to 1500 B.C. The formula for glass is still essentially what it was then, but with refinements and variations, and advanced techniques of manufacture, the glassmakers of modern time have achieved wonderful effects of color, shape, and ornamentation.

Kinds of Antique Glass

Soda (or Soda-Lime) Glass is the oldest and simplest of the glass formulas. The crude form known as bottle glass or green glass has a brown or green tint, depending on the metallic oxides added to the batch. It was used for bottles, window panes, and other household items.

A clear and colorless soda glass was obtained by using more refined materials—soda and bicarbonate of lime—with the addition of black oxide of manganese, or "glassmakers soap."

Flint Glass, or lead glass, unsurpassed for its clarity and brilliance, was obtained from a formula using potash and oxide of lead. It fused at lower temperatures, with a resulting plasticity that made it easy to manipulate, cut, and engrave.

Lime Glass is a leadless glass developed during the Civil War, when lead was scarce. It was cheap to make, requiring bicarbonate of soda and new proportions of lime and other ingredients. Though bright and clear, this glass is neither as resonant nor as heavy as flint glass.

To obtain *colored glass,* makers added the oxides of various metals to the batch: cobalt for blue, copper and iron for green, manganese for amethyst and purple. Red

Top left: Blown glass sugar bowl is engraved and has clarity characteristic of flint glass. Top right: Blown vase and ball stopper of tinted glass. Opposite: Engraving of glass house shows melting-furnaces and blowers working molten glass.

and opaque white were rare before 1830. Glass was also colored by *flashing*—coating with a film of colored glass, and by *staining*—applying a colored stain to the outer surface.

HOW GLASS IS MADE

Glass is produced by the fusion, under extreme heat, of certain purified raw materials. The formula calls for sand (silicon dioxide) as the chief ingredient, an alkali such as soda or potash to lower the melting point, and lime as a stabilizer. This mixture, called a batch, is put into white-hot clay pots and melted in a furnace called a calcar. The molten glass, called the metal, is then shaped into the desired object, either by one of several molding processes, or by manipulation after being bubbled out from the end of a blowpipe. The piece is reheated in an annealing oven and cooled slowly to keep it from becoming brittle.

Glassmaking Methods

Blown Glass has been made by much the same technique since ancient times. A gather of the metal is bubbled out from the end of a blowpipe, and, while supported on the pontil or punty rod, is shaped by the glassmaker using shears, tongs, and other tools to spread, constrict, cut, and elongate the bubble of glass. Blown glass often shows a pontil mark, the scar left when the pontil rod is broken away from the finished piece. **Mold-Blown,** or **Pattern-Molded, Glass** was made between 1820 and 1840. Here the molten glass was blown into the open end of a mold scaled down from the size of the finished piece. After taking the shape of the mold, it was removed and blown to full size, thus enlarging the ribbed, swirled, or quilted pattern received from the mold. Molds varied from simple, open-top dip molds to molds of two, three, and four hinged leaves.

Glass pieces produced by different methods. From left: Vase and glass were blown; flask of chestnut shape was pattern-molded; decanter and stopper were blown in three-section mold; celery vase was pressed (in Ashburton pattern).

Blown Three-Mold Glass, produced by a refinement of the mold-blown technique, was considered a substitute for the English and Irish imports cut off by the War of 1812. The glass was blown into full-size metal molds, usually of three leaves. Most favored were geometric patterns imitating cut glass, and baroque combinations of scrolls, petals, and shells. Molded glass of all types may be recognized by the seam marks of the mold sections.

Pressed Glass, introduced in the 1820's, was the first radically new method of glassmaking in modern times. A mechanical plunger forced the molten glass into the mold, from which the patterned piece was removed in an almost finished state. The product of this fast and economical process was thicker and heavier glass than the mold-blown. It is still plentiful due to its durability and the long period of its manufacture.

Early Glassmakers

Styles in American glass in the 1700's were set by three important makers: Wistar, Stiegel, and Amelung, all of whom employed skilled, European-trained craftsmen.

WISTAR: Between 1739 and 1780, the factory of Caspar Wistar in Salem (then called Wistarberg), N.J., produced bottles, window glass, and a variety of other household articles. It probably originated the glass style called **South Jersey,** characterized by thin threading around the neck and lily pad decoration, an effect obtained by "pulling up" a layer of molten glass over the lower portion of the piece.

STIEGEL: Perhaps the most ambitious glassmaking venture of the 18th century was that of a young German immigrant, William Henry Stiegel, who imported highly skilled blowers, engravers, and enamelers from Europe and England to his factory in Manheim, Pa. From 1763 until its financial failure in 1774, the Stiegel works set styles that influenced glassmakers as far west as Pittsburgh and Ohio. The variety of wares included soda glass; flint glass in glowing shades of blue and purple; molded pieces with ribbed, swirled, fluted, and quilted patterns; and engraved and enameled pieces. Stiegel-type glass is rarely found on the market; the costliest pieces are documented as coming from the Manheim factory.

AMELUNG: In Frederick County, Md., the New Bremen Glass House of John Frederick Amelung did work of outstanding craftsmanship between 1785–95. Amelung was the only glassmaker of the period to sign and date his work, much of which was engraved and made to order as presentation pieces. Amelung glass is important for its influence on later glassmakers. It is practically unavailable, but the glass enthusiast can see it in museum collections.

Distinctive pieces of early-American glass. Right: South Jersey bowl with lily pad decoration (above), and quilted-pattern Stiegel sugar bowl (below). Far right: Amelung goblet with highly detailed engraving of hunting scene.

Bottles and Flasks

Bottles were the first glass products made in America. Shards turned up at the site of Jamestown indicate that glass bottles were being made by even the earliest colonists. In time, bottles were produced in sizes from half-pint to thirty quart. They were made to hold everything from spirits and snuff to shoe blacking, pickles, and perfume; they were shaped for carrying in pockets, saddlebags, and freight cars. Collectors delight in their novelty and historical interest, as well as their generally moderate prices.

Flasks (*/***)—for liquor—came in pint and half-pint sizes, were flat, broad, and short-necked, and could be carried easily in the pocket. Long-necked flasks were considered bottles; handled ones, jugs. Early ones were blown and pattern-molded in both aqua bottle glass and clear glass.

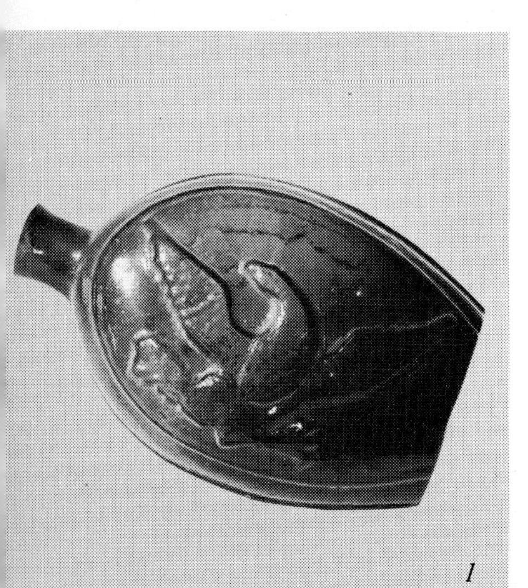

1

2

3

4

Pictorial whiskey flasks appeared after 1820. Favored were portrait flasks of such well-known figures as Washington, Franklin, and Jenny Lind. Patriotic slogans were popular, such as "Pike's Peak or Bust." Later flask designs featured flags, eagles, cornucopias, wheat sheaves, and Masonic emblems. Flasks are still plentiful, but rare ones are in the Expensive bracket. Beware of reproductions.

Perfume Bottles (*/**) are delightful for their diversity. Rare now are the early Stiegel bottles, small enough to be tucked into a lady's glove, and the little South Jersey striped glass seahorse bottles with curled tails. But Victorian bottles—of art glass, cut glass, and even pressed glass—are still easy to find. Bottles for smelling salts and for dressing table use are also in this class.

Bitters Bottles (*) a phenomenon of the later 1800's, were used for carrying a "tonic" of high alcoholic content. They came in pint size and larger, and were labeled or impressed with names such as Traveller's Bitters, Tippecanoe, and Indian Queen.

Figural Bottles (*) from 1870 through the early 1900's, were a popular form of packaging for such products as perfume, liquor, medicine, mineral water, vinegar, and candy. Represented on the list of more than 700 named figural bottles are Moses, George Washington, and Carry Nation; creatures such as fish, turtles, owls; and such miscellaneous objects as pretzels, clocks, and pistols. Like bitters bottles, they are novelty items, of little value for the glass itself.

Apothecary Bottles (*) used in old-time drugstores for storing drugs, were blown in colorless, blue, or brown glass. Standing 7 to 12 inches high, they have ground glass stoppers and the name of the drug, usually in gold lettering, on the side.

1. Mold-blown eagle flask of dark green glass. 2. Blown bottle, paneled, probably for holding snuff. 3. Perfume bottles of painted Bristol glass, ruby glass, ribbed crystal. 4. Bottle in shape of fish.

Pressed Pattern Glass

SANDWICH GLASS (**/***) In 1826, the Boston & Sandwich Glass Co. was established at Sandwich on Cape Cod by Deming Jarves, the son of a Huguenot immigrant, employing skilled workers from Ireland, England, and Belgium. The products of this venture were of superior quality and included almost every type of glass article in demand at the time. The triumph of the Sandwich factory was the *"Lacy Sandwich"* style. This was a pressed pattern flint glass that achieved some of the brilliance of cut glass by refracting light through tiny, closely-spaced stipples that covered most of the outside surface as a background for the central design. More than 1,000 patterns and variants of lacy glass are listed, many of them imitations from factories other than Sandwich. Its period of vogue was the 1830's. Lacy glass is available, but prices run high. Favorite collectibles are the small "cup plates" on which people set their teacups while, as custom had it, they drank their tea from the saucer. Colored pieces are rare.

Above left: Ornate pattern on background of ribbed and stippled glass gives brilliant effect to Lacy Sandwich compote. Goblets are in well-known patterns (from left): Daisy & Button, Wild Flower, Stippled Star, Lincoln Drape.

OTHER PRESSED PATTERN GLASS (*/***) The production of pressed pattern glass flourished for some 70 years. One authority lists more than 2,500 patterns and variants of matching tableware. The earliest pressed glass is the most graceful, especially the classic and restrained flint glass patterns made between 1830–60 by Bakewell, Pears & Co. of Pittsburgh, with names like Argus, Prism, Saxon, and Horn of Plenty. McKee & Brothers of Pittsburgh, The New England Glass Co., and the Boston & Sandwich Glass Co. were other major producers. The delicately ribbed Bellflower pattern, made in the 1850's at Sandwich and other early glass factories, is outstanding. As the century progressed, more opaque glass was used, and also colors, including canary, apple green, emerald green, and electric blue. Glass patterns became ornate during the Civil War years. Then, for the Centennial of 1875, glassmakers created patterns of a decidedly American flavor; the Log Cabin, the Liberty Bell, Westward Ho, and the American Shield pattern are some from this period. In the 1880's and 90's pressed glass went baroque.

Cut Glass

The technique of glass cutting, in which the pattern is deeply incised with grinding wheels and abrasives, reached the U.S. from Germany and England in the early 1800's. It was promptly imitated by pressed-pattern manufacturers; the real thing is recognized by deeper incisions, sharper edges, and heavier flint glass. Pieces are often marked with the maker's name.

Cut glass is one of the best buys on today's market, with more than 100 patterns to look for. The finest pieces, with deep, clear, all-over designs, belong to the so-called Brilliant Period, 1880-1915. Prices are rising, which is understandable considering the quality of this glass. Items range from knife rests or salt dishes (*) to tall vases and punch bowls (**/***).

Paperweights

A single paperweight can bring several thousand dollars at auction, and not unreasonably, for many are masterpieces of the glassmaker's art. The French weights

of the 1840's and 50's inspired master glassmakers in the U.S. throughout the later 1800's, notably Nicholas Lutz and Joseph Galliland, whose flint glass globes enclosed glass fruit, flowers, and millefiori. The Millville Rose, made by Ralph Barber of Whitall, Tatum & Co., N.J. (1905-1912), is probably the pièce de résistance of American weights. Each piece encloses a perfect glass rose in deep rose, pink, white, or yellow.

A collector can take satisfaction in weights less rare and exquisite than these, however. Many of the more available pieces (*/**) are outstanding for their beauty. Prized among the older weights are those with millefiori, latticino, bubbled, Venetian, and candy-striped designs, and Victorian weights with sentiments such as "Home, Sweet Home," "Remember Me," and "Friendship." Many recent weights are worth collecting, especially among the commemorative sulphides enclosing images of notables in silvery relief. The time to buy an outstanding weight, no matter what its age, is now. But outstanding weights of both early and recent vintage are being imitated, so beware of reproductions.

Above left: Cut glass dish in the brilliant Russian pattern. Center: Group of art glass paperweights from the Durand factory. Right: "Millville Rose" weight, a type made in New Jersey between 1905 and 1912.

Glass Favorites

Milk Glass (*/**) is an opaque pressed glassware, usually of a milk-white color, although some pieces are found in blue, green, black, and sometimes pink. It was heavily produced in the 1880's, often pressed in the same molds used for clear pattern glass. Much has survived: tableware of all kinds, figural covered dishes, candlesticks, lamps, and ornamental pieces. It is being widely reproduced and collectors must be cautious. Rely on a trusted dealer, or on long experience in handling it and making comparisons.

Coin Glass (**/***) is an expensive glass of limited availability. When, in 1892, the Central Glass Co. of Wheeling, W.Va., used real coins in pressed-pattern molds, the government charged it with counterfeiting

Left: Figural covered dish of white milk glass. Center: End-of-Day mottled jar. Right: Group of coin glass pieces includes lamp, toothpick holder, mug.

and closed down production after only five months. The pattern had been used for tableware and lamps. Do not confuse this glass with Colombian Coin Glass, which was made with South American coins and is not so expensive.

End-of-Day, Spatter, or **Splashware** (*) is a type of glass named for its mottled appearance, the result of being blown from batches containing bits of colored glass. Popular between 1885 and 1905, it can now be found in ornamental pieces and in useful items such as sugar shakers, mugs, lamps, pitchers, and tumblers.

Holly Amber (***/****) a pressed glass in a holly pattern, was made in Greentown, Ind., for only one year, 1903, after which the factory was destroyed by fire. Thus it is rare and exorbitantly expensive. It has a rich amber color with opalescent bands and panels.

Cranberry Glass (**) is a clear, pinkish-red glass obtained by adding oxide of gold to the batch. It was popular in the 1880's here and in England, where it was called "rose red" and was produced in whole table services, much of which is now on the American antiques market. Cranberry was usually simple in design, but cut, threaded, and decorated pieces may also be found. There are inferior imitations: flashed or stained pieces, and a glass of a ruby-red color made by adding copper to the batch. There is still plenty of true Cranberry available, however.

Mary Gregory (**/***) a ware conceived from a Bohemian painted glass style, was popular in the 1870's and 80's. It was named for the artist—a worker in the Sandwich factory—who set the style for the American version. These pieces of clear, sometimes colored, glass were handpainted with white enamel figures, usually of children at play. Vases, the most common collectible, are usually sold in pairs. Available.

Carnival Glass (*/**) so-called because it was a give-away at carnivals and fairs during the early 1900's, is also called Taffeta Glass and Poor Man's Tiffany. It was made in great quantities after Harry Northwood of Wheeling, W.Va., developed a cheap way to iridize glass. Carnival was pressed in a number of patterns and colors (marigold, purple, dark green, or, more rarely, red or white). Northwood pieces are marked with an "N". Available in quantity, but popularity is forcing prices steadily higher.

There are many other small glass collectibles in the Inexpensive bracket:

Knobs Furniture, door, and mirror knobs. Also curtain tie-backs in many kinds of fine glass, especially clear and opalescent Sandwich Glass.

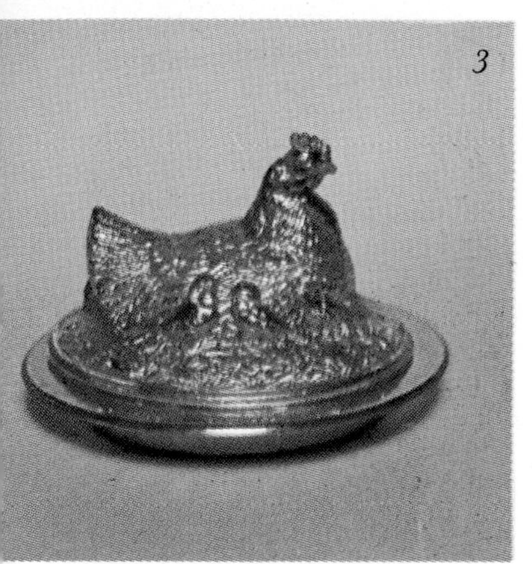

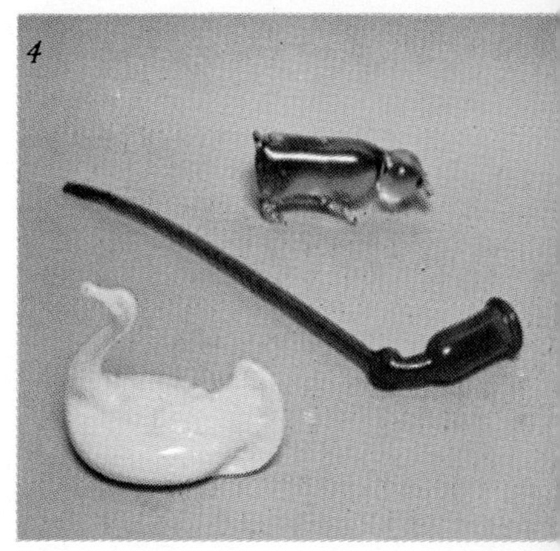

Easter Eggs Some in art glass, but more usually in milk glass, handpainted and decorated with appropriate sentiments.

Whimsies Unusual and sometimes useless pieces by which the glassmaker demonstrated his skill, such as glass hats, shoes, rolling pins, canes, linked chains, hatchets, and miniatures.

1. Cranberry glass pitcher has clear glass handle; bowl has iridescent feet. 2. Mary Gregory barber's bottle. 3. Hen covered dish of carnival glass. 4. Green glass pig, blue pipe, opaque glass bird are "whimsies."

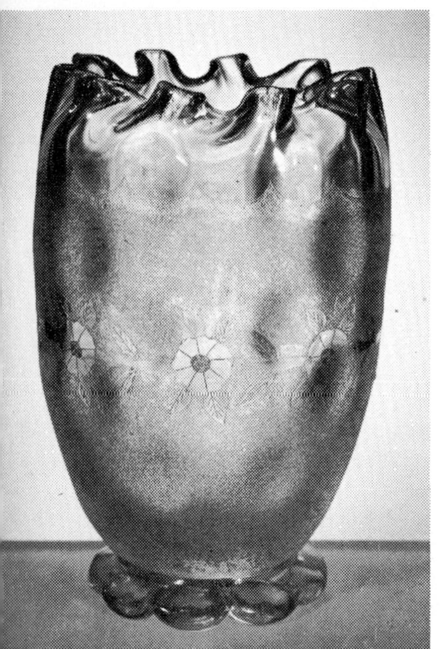

Top: Delicately "cased" Satin glass bowl has lining of darker color glass than outside layer. Above left: Pomona vase gets frosted effect from thousands of small, finely incised curlicues. Above right: Vasa Murrhina urn.

Art Glass

Art Glass, or Fancy Glass, came into its own in America between 1880 and 1910, a period when Victorian baroque was giving way to the flowing, serpentine lines of Art Nouveau. Glassmakers achieved fantastic effects of color, pattern, texture, shape, and decoration, and at the same time produced pieces of elegant simplicity. Most art glass is ornamental, but some useful things, like tableware, scent bottles, and inkwells, may be found. Of the 20 or more types of American-made art glass, the six that follow are of great interest to collectors.

Satin (**/***) This matte-finished glass is noted for its glowing, often shaded colors; it is sometimes lined with contrasting glass. **Pearl Satin,** or **Mother of Pearl,** is a variation with a lustrous finish. Satin glass is not hard to find, nor is it as expensive as other art glass.

Pomona (**) A frosted glass etched with motifs of flowers, berries, leaves and vines; the etching usually is stained yellow. Most pieces show a faint band of amber around the rim. Though not too popular in its day, it is now highly prized.

Vasa Murrhina (**) Often called Spangle Glass, it is a transparent ware in which pieces of colored glass and flakes of mica are embedded. Available.

Peachblow (***) A glassware of simple lines and delicate shading in either a matte or a glossy finish. It is also known as Peach Bloom, Peach Skin, and Coral. Often decorated with gold or enamel, the shading from top to bottom varies according to the maker: Mt. Washington Glass Co.'s is colored from deep pink to blue; Hobbs, Brockunier & Co.'s (from Wheeling) from rose red to yellow in a clear glass with white opaque lining; New England Glass Co.'s, called Wild Rose, shades from rose to white.

Burmese (***) In its subtle shading from salmon pink to creamy yellow, this rich-looking, translucent glass resembles Peachblow. It may be decorated or plain, have a matte or glossy finish. First produced by the Mt. Washington Glass Co. in 1885, it was a favorite with Queen Victoria and was later made in England.

Amberina (**/***) Notable are the metallic ring and the ruby color of the upper portion of this clear, yellow-amber glass. Variations are: Plated Amberina—a ruby-gold Amberina lined with opalescent glass and often seen in ribbed patterns—and Rubena Verde, with the color "flashed" on.

IRIDESCENT ART GLASS

A metallic sheen in a golden or rainbow-like film characterizes this glass, of which there are at least five important varieties.

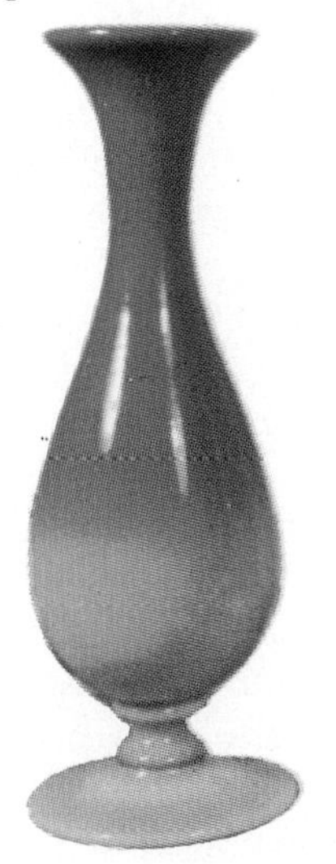

Varieties of art glass (from left): Peachblow vase; Burmese fairy lamp with matte finish; iridescent Tiffany Favrile vase in morning glory shape; group of Durand productions, including iridescent vase with "hooked feather" design.

Tiffany "Favrile" (**/***) L. C. Tiffany, son of the founder of the famous jewelry firm, described his blown Favrile glass as "distinguished by certain remarkable shapes and brilliant and deeply toned colors, usually iridescent." The colors of these ornamental pieces, made between 1890 and 1910, are exotic blendings of blue, gold, and green, and the shapes are inspired by the naturalistic lines of Art Nouveau. Tiffany made other kinds of iridescent and art glass, and he usually marked his work with his name and initials. Pieces added to the Favrile line had that word etched into the base or else a paper label attached.

There were other iridescent glasswares: **Quezal,** often marked; **Durand,** which, if marked, usually has the name or monogram with a large V; **Aurene,** made by Frederick Carder of the Steuben Glass Works, with gold dominating in the iridescent film; and **Kew Blas,** which is hard to identify unless marked.

Glass collector's items sparkle on sunny window shelf.

CARE AND DISPLAY OF GLASS

Glass is at its best when displayed against light, as on window shelves. Closed cabinets should be lighted with concealed bulbs.

To make glassware sparkle wash it in a weak solution of detergent and ammonia. Stains can often be eliminated by soaking in vinegar, washing soda, or household bleach. Crusted sediment can be loosened by adding some old shot, ball bearings, or chain to a cleaning solution and shaking it inside the piece. However, glass that has turned cloudy ("sick") is beyond redemption.

Mending is easier than ever with the improved transparent cements that are now available. Nicked edges can be ground smooth, and some badly nicked or broken pieces can be cut down to advantage.

GLOSSARY

Acid Finish: A dull finish obtained with an acid wash; e.g., frosted glass.

Applied Decoration: Any decoration added to the body of the piece, such as leaves, flowers, trailing vines. Usually in glass of contrasting color.

Blank: A piece of undecorated glass made to be cut or ornamented later, perhaps by another maker.

Bull's Eye: A thick pane of glass with a swirled pontil mark in the center.

Camphor Glass: Acid-finished glass with a cloudy color like gum camphor.

Clam Broth: Cloudy glass with a gloss.

Crystal: Any glass (but usually flint glass) that imitates the exceptional clarity of rock crystal, a natural mineral.

Enameled Glass: Glass decorated with paint fused to the body of the piece.

Acid Etching: A decorative technique in which the pattern is delineated by the corrosive action of acid.

Mercury Glass: A silvery-looking effect made by lining a thin, clear body of glass with a flashing of mercury.

Millefiori: Meaning "thousand flowers." An effect obtained by binding together thin, colored rods of glass, cutting them into wafer-like cross sections, and embedding these in a body of clear, solid glass. Seen in paperweights, doorknobs, etc.

Opalescent Glass: A milky-looking glass obtained by the addition of heat-sensitive minerals to the batch.

Opaque Glass: A term covering various types of non-transparent glass, including Milk Glass, Marble Glass (Slag), Caramel, and Custard Glass.

Overlay: A decorative technique in which one or more layers of glass are cut through to show the inside layer of the piece, often in contrasting color.

Sick Glass: Has turned cloudy with age.

Pottery & China

There are exciting possibilities for collecting in the field of pottery and china. Collectibles range from sturdy pots and crocks, through earthenware china, to fine porcelain, with many pieces carrying their maker's mark. Prices vary according to quality and availability, and there is plenty to be had at moderate cost. American wares predating 1850 will be mostly earthenware, as little American porcelain was made before then.

The basic ingredient of all ceramic ware is clay, of which there are many types. To make china or porcelain, certain rare clays are mixed and refined to obtain a "paste" that is shaped and then fired in a kiln. It is the consistency of the clay or paste that gives a finished piece its characteristic qualities.

Hard paste, the material of which porcelain is made, is mixed of rare clays: kaolin (china clay), and petuntse, a clay containing feldspar. It fuses at very high temperature, producing a vitrified, highly translucent body that does not require a glaze.
Soft paste *is composed of commoner clays and fires at a lower temperature than hard paste. The product is sometimes called artificial porcelain. Since it is permeable, it takes decoration well, but requires a glaze. It is light in weight, but not as translucent as hard paste.*
Glaze *is a shiny, glass-like coating that makes a piece impervious to moisture, strengthens it, and brings out the color. Glazes can be opaque or transparent, colorless or tinted. They can be added to the fired piece or fired with the body in one operation for a vitrified effect. Pieces may be decorated before glazing (underglaze) or after (overglaze).*

POTTERY belongs to the broad category of earthenware—that is, everything made of common clay. It is opaque and usually porous until glazed. It may be shaped completely by hand, or on a potter's wheel (a round platform that spins the clay as the potter molds it with his fingers into a rounded body).
CHINA, a term that came into use during the early importation of porcelain from China, may mean (a) in general usage, any kind of crockery; or (b) in its specific sense, porcelain only. These days, however, authorities prefer to avoid confusion when speaking of porcelain by using that term rather than "china."
PORCELAIN (from the French "porcelaine"—shell) is hard-paste china at its best, with superior qualities

of whiteness, translucence, and hardness. European attempts to imitate Chinese porcelain were not notably successful until 1710, when a deposit of kaolin was found in Germany. English attempts led in the 1790's to the development of "bone china" by Josiah Spode. He added bone ash to the paste, obtaining a handsome china that combined the desirable qualities of porcelain and soft-paste wares.

SEMIPORCELAIN is not porcelain, but a hard, thin, dense stone china (see page 92). It is not translucent and requires a glaze.

American Earthenware

The first ceramics made in America were primitive pots and dishes for household use. It was not until after the War of 1812 that pottery flourished as an industry. Freed of England's restrictions, potters set out to produce wares that would compete with the imports. Though much of this early ceramic production has been lost or damaged, enough remains to provide continuing interest for collectors.

Redware is the name given to the earliest American pottery, made from red clay or clay that turned reddish in firing. Being porous, it was often lead-glazed, especially the inside of vessels. Designs were sometimes incised. It was most abundant in regions offering the proper clay: New York, New Jersey, Pennsylvania, and parts of New England. The pottery of the American Indians is of this character, with primitive decorations repeating tribal symbols.

Slipware (**) is a slip-decorated redware. The slip, a creamy clay, was applied with a tube or quill, much as icing is put on a cake. Most American slipware emanated from the Pennsylvania Dutch country,

1868

though some also came from New England. Perfect pieces are rare.

Sgraffito (**/***) is a scratch-decorated earthenware, the reverse of slipware. It was fully coated with slip and the designs then incised on the clay body through the tacky slip. It was almost exclusively the work of Pennsylvania artisans, who used it as "fancy" ware or to commemorate family occasions. Dated and signed pieces are especially prized.

Rockingham (*/**) is the mottled, brown-glazed earthenware made countrywide between 1825 and 1900. Much came from Norton & Fenton of Bennington, Vt., often marked and dated. This factory also made **Flint Enamel,** a variation of Rockingham with a multicolored, streaked appearance achieved by sprinkling powdered oxides in the glaze. A feature of Rockingham ware is the use of figures for ornamental effect: hound-handled pitchers, coachman bottles, Toby jugs (a roly-poly gentleman whose tricorn hat forms the crown of the jug), and teapots with Rebecca-at-the-Well relief. Unmarked Rockingham is found in kitchenware items, such as mixing bowls and cake pans.

Majolica (*/**) is a brilliantly colored, fancifully shaped earthenware, produced here after 1850. It is metallic glazed and sometimes lined with a pinkish coating. Much is marked, especially the wares from E. B. Bennet (Md.), and the Etruscan majolica from Griffen, Smith & Hill (Pa.); there is also much English majolica on the market. Quality varies. Much of it was made for premium or giveaway use.

Top: Slipware decorated in typical fashion. Middle left: Dated sgraffito plate shows why this pottery is also called tulipware. Middle right: Monkey teapot in Rockingham ware. Bottom: Majolica pieces in typical naturalistic designs.

Stoneware (*/**) is a heavy, nonporous ware that only superficially resembles earthenware. It is actually a hard paste that has vitrified in firing. Its glaze is dull and rough, the result of salt being thrown into the kiln at the peak heat of firing. It is found scratch decorated, or painted in cobalt blue, and sometimes with shallow relief figures. Early pieces of this durable ware are still plentiful, especially jugs and crocks.

Deldare (*/**) made in Buffalo, N.Y., c. 1908, has a rich, olive green earthenware body and underglaze decorations, depicting such scenes as Indian life, the hunt, or "olde England." It was made for table, dresser, and commemorative uses, and is now increasingly collected.

Dedham (*/**) a decorative pottery made in Dedham, Mass., c. 1895, has blue crackling in the glaze and naturalistic border decorations of which a rabbit design was most popular. Available, but in strong demand.

ART NOUVEAU WARES (*/**) These featured the flowing lines and naturalistic shapes of the French style for which they are named. The first American-made Art Nouveau ware was **Rookwood,** c. 1880–1920. It was the creation of Mrs. Maria Storer of Cincinnati, Ohio, who worked with a staff of fine artists. Very distinctive are the Rookwood pieces handpainted under a double glaze, having the effect of a painting seen under water. Marks used were "Rookwood Pottery," "RP," or Mrs. Storer's initials, "MLS." Available.

Other Art Nouveau wares were **Louelsa** (c. 1896) from Weller of Zanesville, Ohio; **sang de boeuf** (ox blood) from the Roseville Pottery, Zanesville, with a red glaze that was slipped to show a lighter color underneath; and **Teco,** from the Gates Potteries, Chicago, Ill. These are all in the Inexpensive bracket.

Top left: Unique "underwater" effect of Rookwood Pottery decoration shows in lidded tobacco jar. Top right: Pitcher from Buffalo Pottery has realistic flowers painted under glaze. Below: Stoneware crock with unusual fruit design.

Early Imports

Many an early American household cherished its Canton or Staffordshire table service. Today imported wares such as these comprise a large portion of what we speak of as American antique china.

CHINESE IMPORTS

From about 1780 to 1840 American merchants and clipper-ship captains carried on a heavy trade in Chinese porcelain. It was made in the inland pottery centers of China (much of it designed for the American market), then brought to port cities for sale.

Canton (**) is a blue and white ware that was exported in great quantities. In fact, its production was discontinued only in the 1950's. This porcelain was free-hand painted under a double glaze with Chinese figures and landscapes. It inspired the ever-popular Willow pattern, still used by china manufacturers in many countries. Canton is readily available.

Chinese Export (or **Trade**) **Porcelain** (***) These wares went for a long time under the name of Chinese Lowestoft, since they were thought to be the product of joint Chinese and English manufacture. Whatever the origin of this view, it has been discredited. Now known as Chinese trade porcelain or Chinese export porcelain, the wares are considered to be of completely Chinese manufacture.

Much of this porcelain was made to order for the European and American market and carried the seals of states or the coats of arms of individuals. Other motifs include flowers, eagles, sailing scenes, and mythological and religious episodes. A peculiarity of Chinese export porcelain is the "orange peel" glaze, so named for its almost imperceptibly pitted surface. It is a popular collectible, available in dinner, tea, and dessert sets, punch bowls, fruit baskets, chamber sets, vases, etc.

Top left: Famille rose exports, like this porcelain bowl, were painted in shades of pink and carmine. Top right: Teapot with emblem has oriental touches in bamboo-turned spout and twined handle. Bottom: Blue and white Canton in three patterns.

ENGLISH IMPORTS

By the early 19th century, the English export trade in china and earthenware, begun a century earlier, was supplying the heavy demands of the American market with wares to please all levels of taste and financial ability. Much of this remains for the collector, with the best buys found among the wares made after 1850.

Historic (or **Old Blue**) **Staffordshire** (**/***) Staffordshire, in England, has long been a pottery center, claiming such makers as Spode, Wedgwood, Minton, Copeland, and Whieldon. The term Staffordshire china, therefore, has broad connotations. But the terms Historic or Old Blue Staffordshire refer to a particular blue-on-white, transfer-printed earthenware produced in the early 1800's by a number of Staffordshire potteries, chiefly Clews, E. Wood, Stevenson, Tam, Mayer, Adams, and Ridgway. Their table and dresser items, designed for the American market after the War of 1812, gained great popularity and later became some of the earliest of favored "china" collectibles.

The characteristic border motifs of each maker (Stevenson—oak leaf and acorns, Wood—seashells, etc.) are a fairly reliable means of identification. The central decoration was usually an American city scene or landscape, often showing some mode of transportation in the foreground, engraved from the drawings of specially commissioned artists. Other designs were portraits and patriotic emblems. This ware was later produced in sepia, black, pink, and green, as well as blue. Historic Staffordshire is available. Collectibles, as indicated by the price symbols, range from the ordinary to extremely choice.

Creamware (**/***) being moderately priced, was perhaps the best seller of the English imports. People

liked the light weight and rich cream color of this simple, lead-glaze earthenware; it was attractive even when bare of decoration. Many potters made it, some with great distinction. Such is the "Queen's Ware" produced by Josiah Wedgwood in the 1760's. Later Creamware collectibles include the pierced, latticework china from Leeds, and black transfer-printed imports from Liverpool featuring emblems, naval scenes, portraits of presidents, and similar motifs. Moderately available.

> ***Transfer printing*** *was a cheap substitute for hand decoration. A design engraved on a copper plate was inked or enameled and then impressed on an extremely thin tissue paper. The tissue, thus printed with the design, was transferred to the glazed piece, which was then refired.*

Left: Historic Staffordshire plate by Enoch Wood shows mill scene on the Brandywine River. Right: Transfer-printed creamware pitcher in familiar pattern, "The Farmers Arms."

Gaudy Dutch (***/****) Gaudy Dutch may be described as an imitation of an imitation. For some time, the potters of Bristol and Staffordshire had been making a porcelain that was a reasonable facsimile of the richly colored Imari china of Japan. Around 1815, they brought out a cheaper, soft-paste version of their imitation; it was colorful, flamboyant, and totally lacking in the formality of the Japanese prototype. This floral-motif "Gaudyware" was rejected by the English market and thereupon diverted to America where it became quite popular, so much so in Pennsylvania that it earned the name **"Gaudy Dutch."** Eleven patterns of Gaudy Dutch are listed: the urn, dove, grape, butterfly, oyster, and six floral designs. Only occasionally available.

Gaudy Welsh (**) a ware made after 1850, was similar to Gaudy Dutch, but harder, heavier, and cruder in design. It often has a bluish-purple coloring with gold or luster touches.

Strawberry (***) another soft-paste Gaudyware, has realistic strawberries painted under the glaze.

Roseware (**/***) c. 1815–65, is a soft-paste, rose-motif Gaudyware in pale colors, with little of the oriental Imari feeling. King's Rose, Queen's Rose, and Adam's Rose are the patterns.

Spatterware (**/***) c. 1820–60, is an earthenware bordered with sponge-applied stippling in red, blue, and green. The central design—of which more than forty are listed—was primitive, showing perhaps a bird, a flower, or a house.

Top left: Roseware tureen and Gaudy Welsh teapot. Top right: Spatterware in Peacock pattern. Middle: Tea set pieces in Strawberry have red berries in raised relief. Bottom: Yelloware, or canary, is often decorated in the gaudy manner.

Willow (*/**) a favorite pattern of English potters since the late 1700's, evolved from the graceful blue-on-white motif of Canton china. European and American versions were of uneven quality; it is the early English marked pieces that have value for collectors.

Mocha (**) c. 1830–50, is an earthenware decorated with brush-dabbed patterns of seaweed, earthworms, trees, cat's eyes, and feathers, in blue, green, tan, red, terra cotta, or black. Often called **Banded Creamware,** it is available, but rarely in perfect condition.

Luster (**/***) c. 1805–1875, (exported to U.S. 1840–1890), is an earthenware, metal-glazed for copper, gold, or silver effects. There are wide variations in shading and design: gold luster over a white ground produced a pinkish-lavender look called "moonlight." Copper lusters, the most popular, could be anything from gold to dark brown. There also were pink and purple lusters. On "resist" lusters the pattern was covered with a

substance that prevented the luster glaze from taking effect. After dipping, the resist was washed off, leaving the pattern in the background color. Stenciled lusters reversed this process; here the piece was completely covered with resist except for the pattern, which finally showed in the luster color against the unchanged background. Lusterware is seldom marked and is of uneven quality, especially the later pieces. Available.

English Delft (**) a favorite since the 1700's, was inspired by Dutch Delft, an earthenware with motifs in blue on milky white and a tin or lead glaze. Some was also made in polychrome. Most available collectibles date from the mid-1800's on.

Old Chelsea (*) a mid-19th century copy of an older Chelsea pattern, is a porcelain with a waxy, soft-white glaze, usually "sprig" decorated (raised reliefs of flowers, grapes, or fleurs-de-lis) in light blue or lavender, often with luster touches.

Opposite page: Old Chelsea teapot (left), and mocha jug with characteristic seaweed decoration (right). Above: Three distinctive pieces of English luster: silver "resist" pitcher, dark copper pitcher, moonlight pattern goblet.

Stone China

Ironstone (*/**) c. 1815–90, got its porcelain-like hardness from the basic materials of earthenware with powdered iron slag added. "Stone china," as first introduced by Spode, Miles Mason, and other English potters, was thin and decorated in the Chinese manner, with much gold. Ironstone later developed into a sturdy utilitarian ware, produced in great variety. Patterns

number more than 200. It was also made with gaudy decoration, and in smooth, pure white, often with raised relief motifs. Also known as granite ware (and incorrectly as semiporcelain or opaque porcelain), it was imported to America in quantity. It is fairly low priced and sufficiently plentiful for collectors to assemble a whole table service of one pattern.

Tea Leaf (*) is a light-weight stone china decorated with "tea leaf" sprigs in copper or gold luster. A notable version of the English import was made by Cartwright Bros. of E. Liverpool, Ohio.

Flow or **Flowing Blue** (*/**) c. 1825, is a Staffordshire stoneware with fanciful and oriental designs printed in deep cobalt blue that was allowed to run in the firing, giving it a washed effect. Available.

Dealers today include in the Flow Blue wares some late English patterns with cloudy flowering and gilt, marked with firm names such as Touraine, and Waldorf. These are a bit cheaper than early Flow Blue.

Stonewares (reading counterclockwise): White ironstone tureen and ladle in wheat pattern, Cashmere-pattern tureen, Flow Blue pitcher, Tea Leaf cup and saucer.

Late Imports

Country	Name	Dates of Import	Mark
Germany	Late Dresden	1875–1900	Crossed swords, Dresden
	Onion	1890–1920	Meissen, crossed swords
	Royal Bonn		Initials FAM, Bonn, Rhein
	Royal Rudolstadt	1854–	Rudolstadt, RW, under crown
	Royal Vienna	1891–	Beehive, Austria
	Royal Bayreuth	1886–	Bayreuth, Bavaria
England	Royal Doulton	1890–	Doulton, Lambeth, England Doulton, Burslem, England
	Royal Worcester	1870–1900	Royal Worcester Porcelain Co.
	Royal Crown Derby	1875–	Royal Crown Derby Porcelain Co.
	Wedgwood	1759–	Wedgwood
Holland	Late Delft	1880–1916	Mark of maker
	Maastricht	1835–1900	Maastricht
Denmark	Royal Copenhagen	1885–	Three wavy lines in blue
France	Haviland	1840–1936	Theodore Haviland, Limoges, France
	Limoges	1850–1900	Limoges and factory mark
Japan	Noritake	1900–	Unmarked or Made in Japan
	Hand-Painted Nippon	1890–1915	Nippon
China	Rose Medallion	1812–1900	Unmarked

Remarks

Patterns are taken from 18th-century designs.
Old Chinese pattern copied by Germany and Denmark; first produced at Meissen.
Rococo and floral motifs.

Floral patterns hand decorated on porcelain.
Copies of early Viennese pieces.
Rose tapestry pattern and novelty pieces.

Sand-colored stoneware with raised design.
Brown- or white-glazed hard porcelain.

Ornate porcelain; floral decoration.

Delicate ware; richly colored Imari designs.
Prized wares are basalt, creamware, and tinted stoneware with classic figures in white relief.

Earthenware with Dutch landscapes and figures in blue on white ground.
Ware resembles English china.

Blue-on-white porcelain; Christmas plates made since 1908.

Fine Limoges porcelain. Delicately decorated with plentiful use of gold.
Comprehensive name for the fine porcelain, hand or transfer decorated, from Limoges factories.

Inexpensive floral china; "azalea" pattern most prized.
Delicate, gold-encrusted china.

Colorful, alternating panels of figures and flowers.

Onion

Limoges

Dresden

Rose Medallion

Top: Representative pieces of Tucker china include vases, pitcher, and fruit dish with gilding and floral designs, and teapot with sepia landscape. Above left: Parian covered dish and bisque figure. Above right: delicately tinted-bisque statuette.

American Porcelain

Except for a few attempts in the late 1700's, there was no fine porcelain made in the United States until 1825. **Tucker** (***/****) c. 1825–38; was one of the earliest and best porcelain wares made in America. The original maker, William E. Tucker, worked with kaolin discovered not far from his Philadelphia workshop and produced a hard-paste porcelain that could withstand extreme heat. Much of this china imitated the fine Sèvres wares of France, with delicate floral designs and much gilt. Tableware pieces of all kinds were made, especially pitchers, as well as presentation pieces. Hulme and Hemphill, names sometimes seen in the markings on Tucker china, refer to a partner and a later owner of the enterprise. This china is available but not in great quantity.

PARIAN (*/**) is an unglazed, molded porcelain, first made by Copeland of the Spode factory in Staffordshire. It was named for its supposed likeness to Parian marble. Much Parian was made in America after 1850, most successfully by Fenton of Bennington, in a variety of decorative and utilitarian wares, including busts, statuettes, and trinket boxes. Vases and pitchers, etc. are glazed on the inside. Decoration is usually in relief, with grapes a favorite motif. Some Parian is colored, such as the **Blue and White** of Bennington.

BISQUE (*/**), meaning "twice baked," is the French term for an unglazed porcelain that had its finest period of production in the 1700's in Europe. American bisque usually appears in parlor ornaments. Those of the Victorian era lacked the fine definition and careful modeling of the earlier pieces. Bisque is available and priced according to quality.

BELLEEK, a translucent, iridescent porcelain, was first made in Ireland around 1857. It was paper-thin but durable. A number of American makers were soon producing American Belleek, which resembled the Irish china but was not as fine in quality. The best is **Lotusware** (***), ornamented with raised reliefs and pierced designs, made by Knowles, Taylor & Knowles of East Liverpool, Ohio, c. 1890–1900. Pieces are usually marked. Most other American Belleek is in the Inexpensive bracket.

HANDPAINTED CHINA (*) usually refers to the commercially produced wares that were handpainted by workers following outlines printed on the plain china. However, another type of handpainted ware is gaining popularity with collectors. In the late 1800's, many ladies made a hobby of painting decorations on plain white china. Examples of their work survive in whole dinner sets, as well as individual pieces, some quite well executed. Prices depend on the quality of the work.

Left: Two examples of Lotusware Belleek are tureen in naturalistic leaf design, and a footed jar more typical of the highly ornate use of shape and ornamentation that distinguish this ware. Right: Idealized painting on Belleek vase is example of Art Nouveau style in American pottery.

CARE AND DISPLAY OF OLD CHINA

Mending: Broken china need not be a total loss. Even if pieces are missing, professionals in china repair can mold new handles, fill in gaps, make cracks invisible, and touch up color in an exact match. Less perfect jobs can be done at home with mending cements, colored enamels, and an ironstone putty for fashioning new parts. No way is known, however, to repair or disguise crazing, a fine crackling of the glaze caused by age and heat.

Cleaning: Most discolored china can be bleached at home by a thorough soaking in household chlorine bleach. If too discolored, give it to a professional.

Display: China plates should be displayed upright. If your shelf or cupboard has no groove for standing the plates, a piece of thin molding nailed to the shelf will do as well. Most pieces can also be hung on hooks or specially designed spring wire gadgets. If china is stored in stacks, place paper pads or doilies between the dishes to prevent chipping and scratching.

Metalware

Silver

Of the collectors' items in metalware, silver is in a class by itself. It is expensive, and early pieces are rarely available. But there is an abundance of 19th century collectibles—small items and plated silver—offering the collector a taste of the artistry that silversmiths of every age have brought to their work.

The treasury of American antique silverware got its start with the extensive silver services brought or ordered from abroad by the wealthier colonists. It grew as native and immigrant silversmiths set up shops in such cities as Boston, New York, and Philadelphia.

Silversmiths worked by hammering the heated metal over a form from which the desired shape was "raised." They finished the piece with repeated annealing and hammering, soldered on bases, rims, handles, etc., then finally polished the whole piece.

QUALITIES IN SILVERWARE

Silver plate originally meant articles of solid silver, the metal being obtained by melting down coins (in Spanish, *"plata"*) taken in exchange for British cargoes in the West Indies and South America. (The term has come to be used for plated silver.)

Coin silver had a silver content the same as English silver coins, 900 parts silver to 100 parts base metal. In the early 1800's, such pieces bore the word "coin."

Sterling (the name of an old English penny) was first stamped on silver in 1850 to show the quality: 925 parts silver to 75 parts alloy.

Silver gilt was an amalgam of gold and mercury electrolytically joined to all or part of a silver piece.

Plated silver is the term for electroplated ware made from 1840 on. In this process, silver is chemically deposited on a metal base. Rogers Bros., Reed & Barton, Meriden Britannia, and others made it in the U.S., and there is much on the market. It is valued according to the depth of the plate (from standard to quadruple), and the taste and execution of the design. It is sometimes worth having resilvered.

STYLES American silver was influenced by contemporary English and European styles, particularly the graceful simplicity of the long Georgian period, 1727–1800. Earlier silver includes examples of the Queen Anne and rococo periods, while the work of many New York smiths has the simple, sturdy lines favored by the Dutch.

In the 19th century, American silver styles first followed classic designs favored during the Federal period, later became ornate in Victorian fashion, and turned again toward simplicity by the end of the century.

Small silver pitcher is embossed, beaded around neck and lip, and engraved. Other embellishments often seen are filigree *(open work) and* gadrooning, *a spiral or rope molding effect used to finish edges.*

MARKS English silver pieces carry a complex hallmark of symbols signifying the maker, his town, the date, and the silver content. Though some American makers marked their work in the same way, the usual manner was a simple maker's mark.

OLD SHEFFIELD PLATE This ware, made of silver welded to copper, dates to the 1740's, when English smiths perfected the welding process as a means of using less silver. The joined metals, in rolled sheets, could be shaped much as solid silver, though edges were usually beaded or otherwise ornamented to conceal the copper filling. Sheffield plate was made in the same styles as the silver of the time, and with no less care. It was not, however, regularly marked by its English makers. Its century of popularity ended in 1840, when the electroplating process was patented. It is available but is almost as costly as solid silver. An

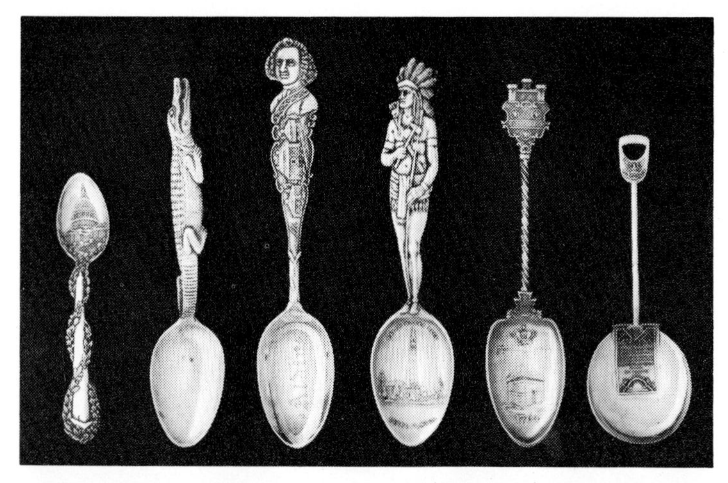

BORDEAUX
BRANDY
CLARET
SHERRY

old piece that shows "bleeding"—the copper exposed by wear—is usually left untouched, as resilvering might spoil the color and patina of the piece.

COLLECTIBLES (*/****) The best buys for the beginning collector include: tableware—flatware, plates, serving dishes, mugs; epergnes; castor sets (for holding glass condiment bottles); pickle castors, often with tongs; souvenir spoons (a late Victorian fad); also sugar tongs, napkin rings, knife rests, trivets, toothpick holders, perfume bottles, vinaigrettes, soap boxes, match boxes, inkstands, flasks, decanter labels, and tea caddies.

CARE Silver must be polished to remove tarnish. Lacquering to prevent tarnish sacrifices the silver's natural patina. Silverware will stay bright longer if displayed in a closed cabinet where a piece of gum camphor has been tucked away.

Pewter

Pewter is an amalgam of base metals, chiefly tin and copper, plus varying amounts of zinc and antimony. Fine English pewter contains no lead; in the softer, common pewter, lead is substituted for copper.

The method of fashioning pewter into tableware, its chief use, was simple. It was either melted and poured into a mold; or, for shallow pieces such as dishes, it was hammered into shape over a form. Later pieces were also turned on a lathe.

Up to 1840, the pewterers' business flourished in America despite low import duties on English-made wares, and heavy duties on the raw tin needed for making pewter. Much pewterware was required for church, home, and tavern use, and it was common for worn pewter to be melted down and recast rather than to be discarded.

A sampling of smaller collector's items in silver (from top): Traveling soap container and sugar tongs; commemorative silver spoons; artistically wrought labels for liquor bottles

Many of the best pewterers were New England men: the Boardman and Danforth families of Connecticut, the Melvilles of Newport, and the Hamlins of Providence. Philadelphia and New York also had fine craftsmen.

STYLES American pewter had a simple, sturdy grace. Unlike the heavily embellished foreign pieces, decoration was largely confined to beaded edges and the pierced designs of porringer handles.

MARKS Pieces usually carry a "touchmark" signifying the maker. Early American pewter is marked in the English manner, with symbols such as an eagle, rose, dove, or ship. Names or initials of the maker were the usual marks of later pieces.

COLLECTIBLES (**/***) Much early American pewter was melted down to make shot for the Revolution and the War of 1812, and what remains of the early ware has a higher market price than English pewter of comparable age, simply because there is less of it. Collectibles include: salvers, porringers, tankards, tea and coffee pots, lamps, candlesticks.

CARE Fine pewter takes a high polish, but many people prefer to leave it dark. The cleaning of pieces turned very black should be left to a professional, as should straightening and mending. Once cleaned, pewter can be kept pleasantly bright with a good commercial pewter polish. "Sick" pewter, hopelessly worn and pitted, is unsalvageable.

Left: Collection of English pewter displayed in Pennsylvania cupboard. Above: American pewter pieces include tankard (1), Federal era teapot (2), teapot in Queen Anne style (3), and shaving mug (4).

Britannia

BRITANNIA, a tin alloy containing little or no lead, was developed in England about 1800. Pieces were "spun" on a lathe by pressing sheets of the metal against revolving forms with blunt tools. The product of this somewhat mechanized approach was a thinner, lighter, more sharp-edged ware than lead pewter. It became so popular that by 1825 it had all but taken the place of pewter for table use in England and was being made in quantity in America also. After 1840 it was used as a base for electroplated silverware.

COLLECTIBLES (**) Favorite pieces are whale-oil lamps, candlesticks, and tea and coffee pots with wooden handles. Washbowls, ladles, measures, and nursery bottles are popular, in addition to the many kinds of articles earlier made in pewter. Much is marked. Among the outstanding makers are Dixon (English), Calder, Boardman & Hart, Trask, Roswell, and Gleason.

Above: Early Britannia ware by English maker, Dixon. Right, reading clockwise: Copper "foot-of-ale" mug, copper document box, brass candlesticks, brass teapot. All are burnished to look their best.

Brass and Copper

Utilitarian articles of brass and copper have seen heavy duty in American households since the early 1700's, most of them either brought by the colonists or imported from England. Not many can be attributed to American coppersmiths, since they lacked the industrial facilities for turning out the finished metals in sheets. Smiths hammered out their own sheets or sent to England for them. Their work, moreover, is hard to recognize since they followed English styles and seldom marked their wares. American pieces tend to be heavier, however, than those made in England, and some have been matched up to their makers with the help of inventory lists and advertisements of the 1700's. Among the colonial artisans were Paul Revere and his pupil, William Hunniman, Richard Lee of Massachusetts, Benjamin Harbeson and Caspar Wistar of Philadelphia, and Frederick Steinman of Lancaster, Pa.

Brass items of lasting utility are oil can with stopper (above) and fireplace jamb hooks (left). Brass scales like that at right are favored for use in home décor.

Early utensils of copper and brass (an alloy of 2 parts copper to 1 part zinc) were shaped by hammering the metal sheets into iron molds. Handles and spouts were riveted on after being carefully shaped to fit. Items such as candlesticks, andirons, and doorknockers were cast in wooden molds.

COLLECTIBLES (**) Many articles were made in both copper and brass, although the latter was favored for such items as doorknockers, buttons, andirons, jamb hooks (for hanging fireplace hardware), mortars and pestles, bedwarmers, clock faces, furniture hardware, and candlesticks. Items to look for in both metals include kettles and pails of all kinds and sizes, coal scut-

tles, coffee pots, chafing dishes, trivets, saucepans, ladles, spatulas, strainers, funnels, scales, measures, bed and foot warmers, tobacco boxes, bells, and weathervanes.

Only the advanced collector or student of antiques will be able to track down the few authentic early American pieces of copper and brass in shops today, but if a piece is of good quality and style, why discriminate? Just beware of brand new items made in the U.S. or abroad. A piece should date to the Victorian period, at least. Despite scarcity, prices in general are not prohibitive: $50 will buy a burnished apple-butter kettle (a Pennsylvania specialty), Chippendale andirons, a warming pan, or a footman (a high trivet).

Iron

Articles of iron were expensive in colonial America. Of the plentiful iron ore resources of the country, the first to yield to the relatively simple tools of the early settlers were the surface bog-iron deposits. Forges and furnaces were few until the period 1700–25, when many sprang up in the Northeast. But much of the iron they produced was exported to England and later imported back to America as finished products. By 1800, however, the domestic production of iron articles was beginning to catch up to the needs of the young nation. Most of the ironware available today is 19th century.

Early iron pieces were hand-wrought or cast in molds. **Wrought iron** is grainy and bears the marks of the forging process, during which the red hot metal was "pulled" and hammered by the smith. **Cast iron** is brittle and hard, and the surface, though smooth, tends to show pitting. By mid-19th century, it had almost entirely replaced wrought iron in domestic production.

Iron, by its nature, lends itself to use in utilitarian articles—tools, utensils, hardware, and machinery. It is the first three categories that interest the collector.

TOOLS AND IMPLEMENTS (*) These include axes, hammers, blacksmiths' tools, and farm implements. Prices are fairly low; a simple tool like a broad axe would cost $7 or $8.

BUILDING HARDWARE (*/***) Very interesting items are available, including shutter hooks, hinges, latches, locks and bolts, door handles and key plates, footscrapers, and fences and railings. Besides age, an important factor in determining the price of an iron piece is imaginative design, as frequently seen in weathervanes and doorknockers.

Fanciful iron building accessories. Top: Running fox weathervane. Bottom, from left: Shoemaker's shop sign and eagle doorknocker, both of early 1800's; ball-and-hand doorknocker of Victorian era.

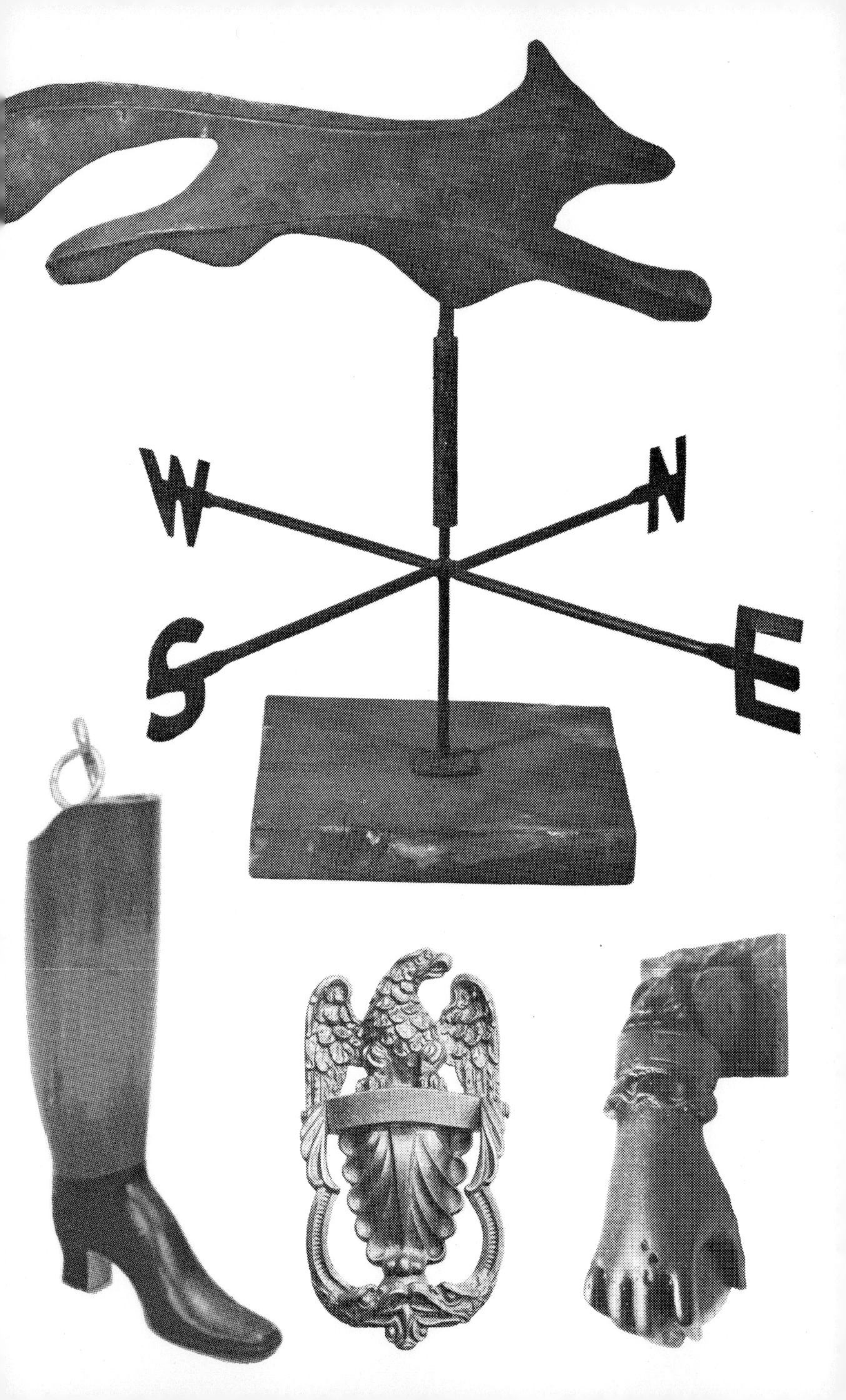
W
N
S
E

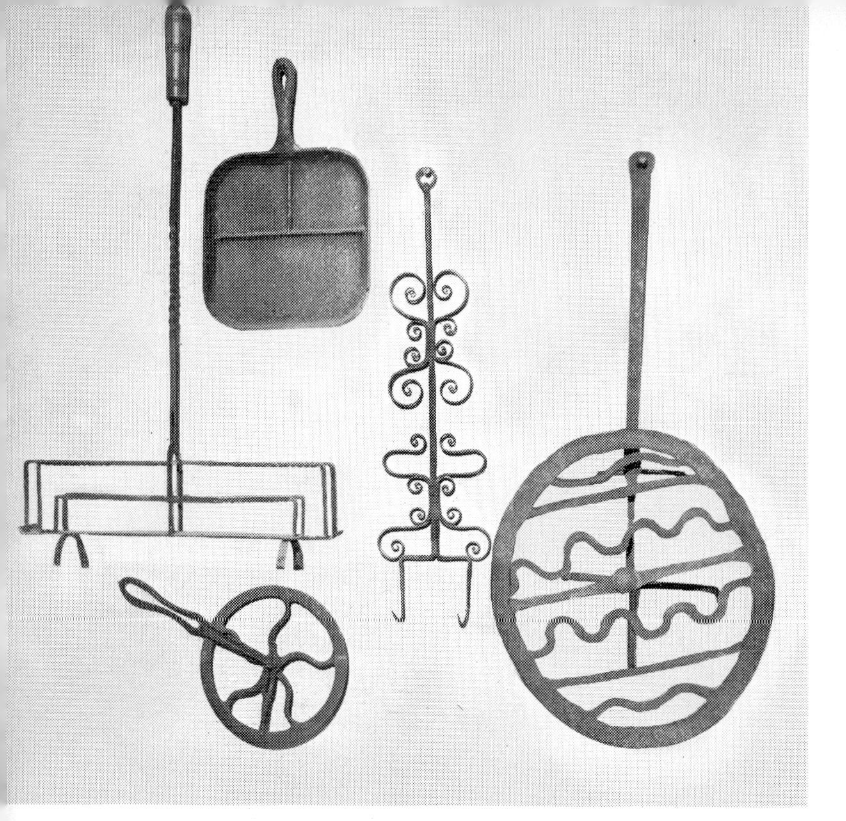

Top: Fireplace cooking equipment, toaster on far left, revolving griddle on right. Above: Victorian boot jack and Hessian soldier andirons of late 1700's.

FIREPLACE EQUIPMENT (*/**) The colonial hearth had an array of wrought-iron implements designed to make it work efficiently in warming the house and cooking the food. Low "fire dogs," a rudimentary form of andiron used in the early 1700's, supported the logs. Later andirons were of cast iron, often in quaint forms such as the Hessian soldiers of the 1780's. Those used in rooms other than the kitchen often had brass finials and other decorative touches.

The kitchen hearth had a crane that swung out from the fireplace wall, with adjustable hooks, or trammels, for hanging pots and kettles from its extended arm. Cooking utensils included forks, ladles, spoons, dippers, toasters, skewers, kettles, skillets, waffle and wafer irons, broilers, trivets, and peels (long-handled shovels for removing cooked food from the brick oven).

STOVES (*/***) Few of the cast-iron "fire plates" or plated "jamb stoves" of the mid-1700's, so admirable for the vigor and simplicity of their relief designs, remain for the collector. Even the Franklin stoves, free-standing, iron-sided fireplaces first introduced in 1742, are now so scarce as to command almost any price. But wood and coal stoves of the 19th century are still available. Now favored are the decorative "parlor" stoves of the 1840's and 1850's (**).

OTHER IRON COLLECTIBLES (*/**) Cast-iron furniture, though expensive, is now much in demand for outdoor use. Miscellaneous smaller items in favor include door stops, boot jacks, trivets, "betty" lamps, hitching posts, and branding irons.

CARE Rust on old iron can be removed with a wire brush and one of the various chemical cleaners on the market. Deepen the hue with black shoe polish, well rubbed in; painting gives an artificial look.

Tin

When the cookstove replaced the open hearth in the early 1800's, tinware became an important item in the American home. The American tradition of the itinerant tin peddler started in 1840 when the wares made by the Pattisons of Berlin, Conn., began to be sold from traveling horse carts. Tinsmiths also became numerous, mostly to fill the demand for kitchenware. Wares of a more decorative sort were made too, especially by Pennsylvania Dutch artisans.

PLAIN TIN COLLECTIBLES Most tinware was made from thin, rolled sheets of tin-plated iron. Utilitarian wares for domestic use (*), such as cookie cutters and candle molds, were quite plain and functional. Semi-decorative accessories (**), including wall sconces, chandeliers, candlesticks, and mirror frames, were also usually unpainted and fairly plain. These old pieces are heavier than later tinware and have a soft, satiny finish. They are easy to find, especially kitchen things.

PUNCHED TINWARE (**) Pierced or indented tinware was especially popular with the Pennsylvania

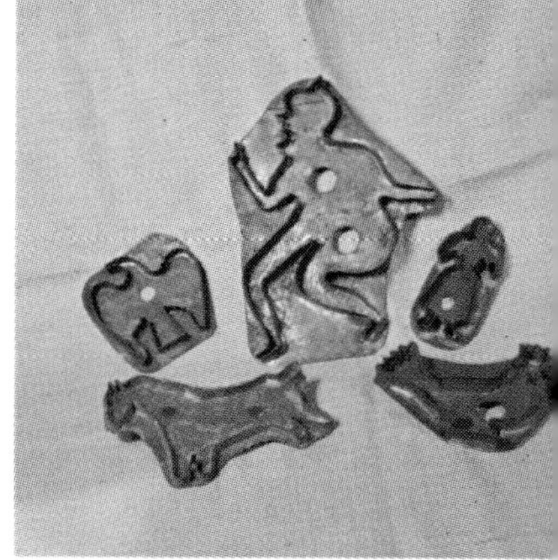

Above left: Tin coffeepot with punched Pennsylvania Dutch designs. Above right: Cookie cutters, including rare eagle and devil designs. Right: Tin kitchenware painted in bold Pennsylvania Dutch motifs.

Dutch. Some articles were pierced for functional reasons, as lanterns to emit light, or footwarmers to give out the warmth of the hot brick within. Many items had designs embossed from the inside, but these are no longer plentiful and are expensive when found.

PAINTED TIN (*/**) took inspiration from the fancy Tôleware of France and the painted Pontypool pieces of England. Flowers, leaves, berries, scrolls, peacocks, and Pennsylvania Dutch motifs were painted in gay colors against a strong background such as flat black, ivory, yellow ocher, vermillion, and indigo blue. Trays, coffee and tea pots, salt and pepper shakers, and boxes of all kinds are the most usual painted items. Stenciled motifs with metallic touches were often combined with hand painting on decorated American tinware of the 18th and early 19th centuries.

New Tôle (*) is a late tinware collectible decorated with transfer printing. Many such items had commercial origins as packaging for cookies or tea, and some are quite handsome.

Primitives

A category of antiques called "primitives" was born out of the artistic expressions of people who lacked formal training in the arts. Two large groups of items are included in this category. First, things of solely artistic purpose—such as portrait paintings and silhouettes; and, second, functional items—such as patchwork quilts, decorative weathervanes, and shop signs—of which artistic touches are an integral part. What these primitives have in common, besides being hand-produced, is their individuality and their freedom from formal style.

Needlework

SAMPLERS (*/**) c. 1700–1850, were considered good practice in the art of embroidery. The alphabet, numerals, flowers, and figures, as well as mottoes and pious verses ("While God doth spare, For death prepare") were stitched in threads of wool or silk. Usually signed with the name of the maker, her age, and the date, samplers of the 1800's are easy to find.

QUILTS (*/**) c. 1750–1860, can be masterpieces of needlework. Early ones were decorated solely by the fancy stitching that held the top, backing, and inner lining together. **Patchwork quilts** were common by 1800. These were made of remnants "pieced" together in geometric designs, or sewn together at random, as in the "crazy quilt." **Appliqué** allowed floral and other curved-line designs. In appliquéd quilts, the material of the design is sewn onto a background of cotton or muslin. Patterns in both appliquéd and patchwork

quilts were a strongly traditional matter. Bear's Paw, Star of Bethlehem, Log Cabin, Drunkard's Progress, and Jacob's Ladder are some of the more than 400 named patterns. Quilts made before 1850 are scarce.
COVERLETS (**) were homemade in colonial days, woven with wool or cotton yarn in three-color, geometric patterns which sometimes showed great variety and subtlety. In the 1800's it became customary to give the home-spun and dyed yarn to professional weavers, who had Jacquard looms capable of weaving the wool on linen warp in reversible patterns and figured designs of buildings, birds, flowers, etc. One-piece coverlets post-date 1830, when the first full-width loom was invented. Coverlets are best found in the East and Midwest, some with the year and the owner's or weaver's name woven into the design; red, indigo blue, green, ecru, and white are the usual colors. They should never be washed, and should be dry cleaned only with care.
FLOOR COVERINGS (*/**) were not common until the 1800's. Of the six or so kinds of homemade rugs that came into use, **hooked rugs**—made of narrow wool strips hooked close together through a backing of linen or burlap—have held up best and are the favorite of today's collector. On some, the loops were cut for a plushy effect. Designs were often original with the maker and range from lettered sayings and geometric patterns

to figures of flowers, animals, birds, and houses. In special demand today are rugs worked in the prepatterned backings designed and sold by Edward Sands Frost, a New England peddler of the 1870's (**).

The collector may come across old braided, button, rag, or chenille rugs, but few are to be found in usable condition. Vacuuming and beating are death to old handmade rugs. They should be swept with a soft brush and the colors freshened with a foam rug cleaner.

Carving

WOOD CARVING was both a familiar pastime and a livelihood for many men in earlier days. Of today's wood-carved collectibles, some are household items, some are decorative and commercial pieces made by unknown carvers, while others, distinguished by their style and vigor, were done by well-known artisans.

Carved **figures**—bird, animal, and human—were done by many primitive carvers, best-known of whom is William Schimmel, who worked in the Shenandoah Valley, c. 1860–90. His angry-looking painted eagles are especially prized collectibles (**/***). Aaron Mounts (a friend and pupil of Schimmel's), Noah Wise of Pennsylvania, and John H. Bellamy of Maine are other carvers famed for their bird and animal figures (**). The work of these men is getting rare, however.

Far left: Alphabet sampler carries name of maker and 1809 date. Left: Intricately woven coverlet has eagle motif favored in 1830's and 1840's. Above: Border of quilt made in Civil War times.

American primitives. Above: Scrimshaw etching on ivory of whaling port. Right, reading clockwise: Watchmaker's sign carved from wood and painted with watch face; 18th-century carved wood statue, standing 18 inches high; intricate piecrust jagging wheel carved from ivory; featherbed smoother with bird handle; chip-carved rack with two drawers for holding spoons; in center, Lehnware cup, example of brightly painted wooden ware made in the mid-1800's by Joseph Lehn of Pennsylvania, popular at the time for gift giving.

COMMERCIAL CARVING was done by artisans for use in connection with business or trade. Such, for example, are the wooden **figureheads** that adorned the bowsprits of sailing vessels, and the **wooden Indians** and other figures so often a feature of old-time tobacconists' shops. Figureheads are now museum pieces, but the collector with about $1,000 to spend can still get a life-size cigar-store Indian.

More moderately priced are **shop signs** made in fascinating shapes, such as boots, watches, spectacles, gloves, candy-striped poles, etc.; (**). Moderately available.

Early **carousel** and **circus figures** also are being keenly sought, with prices running to $250 or more.

SCRIMSHAW (**) c. 1790–1840. Carved, needle-etched articles made from whale bone and walrus tusk, were a sailor's pastime. Snuff boxes, busks (corset boards), pie crust jagging wheels, watch holders, chess sets, jackstraws and other toys, cane handles, and small figures are all available, especially in New England.

& CO.

Painting

PRIMITIVE PAINTINGS (***/****) were the work of untrained but gifted artists. Though characterized by rigid composition, distorted perspective, and naive treatment of subject matter, these paintings have a vitality, freshness, and color that qualify them both as art and as collectors' items. Most of the artists are unknown, though some did achieve reputations, such as Edward Hicks, Erastus Field, and Ruth Henshaw Bascom.

The 19th century, before the invention of photography, was the most fertile period for American primitives. Still lifes, landscapes, ship scenes, and scriptural and historical episodes were painted in oils and watercolor by many amateurs, as well as by the itinerant painters whose stock in trade was individual and family portraits.

A primitive of the Spanish-settled Southwest is the **santo,** a saint's likeness painted on tin or wood (*/**). FRACTUR was a style of watercolor illumination practiced by the Pennsylvania Germans in the 18th and 19th

Left: Hearts, tulips, "hex" designs provide color in piece of Pennsylvania fractur. Center: Primitive painting shows bridge at Harpers Ferry. Right: Reverse painting of city scene is from tablet of Empire-style clock.

centuries. Certificates of birth, baptism, and marriage, house blessings, bible records, and scriptural quotations are some of the items that were illuminated with hand-painted angels, birds, flowers, and other Pennsylvania Dutch motifs. Early examples are still available (**), but less so than later fractur, c.1860–80 (*), on which motifs were printed in outline, to be completed with hand lettering and sometimes hand coloring.
REVERSE PAINTING ON GLASS (**) came into vogue about 1820. Here, a picture is painted in reverse on one side of a pane of clear glass, so as to be viewed from the other side; an overlay coat of white or pastel provides a background for the colors. The usual subjects were portraits, landscapes, and religious themes, and the artists were mostly unknown. Available (often on mirror frames and clock panels), but not common.
COMMERCIAL PAINTING is the work done on coaches, shop and inn signs, etc., by men who called themselves "House, Sign and Fancy Painters." Much of it is admirable and has been acquired by museums, but later-19th century pieces can still be found (**/****).

MINIATURES (**), painted both by amateurs and by trained artists, were cherished personal remembrances in the 19th century. (Signed pieces by professional artists are not "primitives"; they belong in the realm of art collecting.) The miniature was meant to be a close likeness, and was usually painted in oils on ivory (which gives a curious luminosity to the paint) or on bone, porcelain, cardboard, or copper. The interest of the average collector will run to unsigned pieces, which are available, though no longer plentiful.

SILHOUETTES (*/**) done from life were something of a fad in the early 1800's. They are of three types: **cut and pasted**—made of a black paper cutout mounted on a white background; **hollow cut,** in which white paper, with the image cut out, is mounted on a black background; and, thirdly, **drawn** or **painted** silhouettes. Some silhouettes were done with great skill and artistry by men like William H. Brown and the French émigré, Augustin Edouart. Thousands more were turned out by itinerant silhouettists, and thus the range of quality and description is very great.

Most silhouettes are bust profiles, but there are many full-length portraits, even family groups. Some have the features, costume, or background lightly sketched in with oils or watercolors. Most choice and expensive are those of famous people, and those by well-known silhouettists, who number close to a hundred. Plenty of silhouettes by anonymous artists are available.

CUTWORK (**) Papyrotamia, the art of cutting flowers, figures, or intricate scenes from black or white paper, was a favorite pastime of 19th-century ladies.

THEOREMS (**) This was an artistic skill taught in young ladies' seminaries c. 1810–40. Paintings were done on velvet with the aid of stencils.

Top left: Carefully executed miniature painting.
Top right: Basket of fruit is subject of theorem, painting on velvet.
Above: Near life-size example of papyrotamia; many-figured, seemingly-dimensional scene is cut from black paper.

Clocks & Lighting

Perhaps it is their self-contained animation that gives clocks a special fascination as collectors' items. The variety available is considerably reduced if foreign clocks are excluded; but, even so, American-made clocks, especially of the 19th century, are plentiful and extremely satisfying, both for their function and their decorative value. The tall, standing GRANDFATHER CLOCK (****), as it came to be called, housing weights and pendulum in a case sometimes 8 feet high or taller, was the first important contribution of colonial clockmaking. The prime period of production for these clocks was between 1770 and 1820, well before the age of mass production. Requiring the skill of both watchmaker and cabinetmaker, they were costly to construct and to buy. In the home they stood as pieces of furniture, and the cases followed prevailing styles: Chippendale to the end of the 18th century, with Hepplewhite, Sheraton, and Empire all following as times and tastes dictated.

The grandfather clock usually has a round dial set in a square face. Often surmounting this is an arched area adorned with either a painted scene, or with moving parts indicating the date or the phases of the moon. Dials are usually painted black on a white background, although brass dials are frequent on older clocks. Furniture woods of all kinds were used for the cases, especially mahogany. Simple cases often were made of pine. Though less frequently signed than the works, the cabinets of grandfather clocks are of greater interest to collectors. The Chandlee family of Philadelphia and David Rittenhouse, also of Pennsylvania, were outstanding makers of tall case clocks. So-called **grandmother clocks** (***/****), often designed as shelf clocks, are half-size versions of the tall clock, standing 3 to 5½ feet high. They were made from 1800 on by many famous makers.

After the Revolution, American clockmakers began to fill the need of the new nation for inexpensive, dependable timepieces.

WALL CLOCKS Both beauty and utility were served by the **banjo clock** (***/****), a type of hanging clock admirable in the economy of its design, first produced by the Willard brothers of Massachusetts (1790–1820). The brass works of the banjo clock ran eight days on one winding. Its round face and rectangular base are connected by a pendulum case some 20 to 26 inches long. The most frequent adornments are gilt scrolling along the sides of the shaft, an eagle finial atop the dial, and painted glass panels in the base and shaft. Many makers made banjo clocks, though the Willards, which are unsigned, are considered the finest. Other shapes used for clock cases were the lyre and the acorn, for both wall and shelf clocks (**/***).

Early American clocks (from left): Grandmother clock, miniature of tall type, stands about 3½ feet high; banjo clock with eagle finial and painted tablet; Eli Terry pillar and scroll-top clock.

SHELF CLOCKS These offered the cheapest timekeeping for early American households. As early as 1808, the Connecticut factories of Eli Terry were using rudimentary mass-production methods to turn out clocks by the hundreds, many of them with wooden works. Terry's **pillar and scroll-top clock** (***), introduced about 1815, became very popular. Standing just under two feet high, the best of these have slender feet, pillared sides, and broken-arch tops. Terry made many other styles of shelf or mantel clocks, as did his close contemporary, Seth Thomas, and others in the thriving Connecticut clockmaking industry.

There are many other styles of shelf clocks from the period 1825–50 (**/***). About 1825, Gothic-style **steeple clocks** appeared, featuring one or two finials rising on either side of a pointed arch above the clock face. Another design of the 1820's was the flatiron-shaped **beehive clock.** The wonder of the 1830's was the **wagon spring clock** by Joseph Ives. Instead of a pendulum and weights, it was moved by horizontal springs, similar in principle to wagon springs. During the 1840's, clock cabinets were made with the ogee (S-shaped) molding and heavy pillars of Empire design. Perhaps the best were by Chauncey Jerome, another Connecticut clockmaker.

A feature of shelf and mantel clocks is the tablet, the small door at the base of the clock, giving access to the pendulum. This is usually fitted with glass and decorated with reverse painting or (after 1840) decalcomanias. Also frequent are mirror tablets, and clear glass tablets that allow the swinging pendulum to be seen.

LATE CLOCKS (*/**) These, from the period 1850–1900 and later, are naturally more available than early timepieces. There is an immense variety in household clocks, from simple oak kitchen pieces to marble mantle clocks and china boudoir clocks, many ornamented in full-blown Victorian fashion. Then there are clocks made for business and institutional use. This field is still well stocked with timepieces displaced by electricity from offices, schoolrooms, post offices, and railroad stations.

PRICES The collector should count on having some work done on any old clock he acquires. In buying, it may be possible to bargain if the timepiece is not working or if the original key has been lost. Prices, however, are not too high, considering the charm of clocks.

Top left: Steeple clock with unusual carving and frosted glass tablet. Top right: Simple Gothic clock with reverse painting on tablet. Bottom: China boudoir clock and walnut kitchen piece from late Victorian period.

Lighting

Between the wrought-iron rush holders of the early settlers and the ornate gas chandeliers of Edwardian days, there exists an immense range of lighting collectibles, most of which are readily adaptable for modern decorative and functional use.

CANDLESTICKS Here there is endless variety. There are plainly functional sticks of tin or pewter, used in the kitchen or other work settings. There are parlor pieces in brass, silver, glass, wood, and china that demonstrate the passing styles as clearly as do furniture and silverware. There are simple sticks for holding one candle, candelabra for two or more, and hanging chandeliers. And there are lanterns and coach lamps for lighting the way out of doors.

An interesting aspect of candlesticks is the variety of features they have for intensifying the light given off. Such are wall sconces of mirrored glass or polished metal, glass prisms, and multiple holders. The scarcity of tallow in pre-whaling days is also evident in the design of many sticks, such as those with a movable socket in the shaft enabling the stump of the candle to be moved up and fully consumed.

FAVORITE COLLECTIBLES: **Chamber sticks** (*), on a saucer-shaped base with a handle, used in colonial days to light the way to bed; **fairy lamps** (**/***), squat 19th-century versions of the chamber stick, with ornate glass shades; **lanterns** (**), including the glass-sided type and the so-called "Paul Revere lanterns" of pierced tin with a conical top; conical-base **petticoat lamps.** Also popular are candle accessories: scissor-like trimmers (snuffers) and conical extinguishers, often in sets with tray (*).

Candlesticks of brass are perhaps the most plentiful, but it is difficult to tell an old stick from a reproduction. Early sticks should be heavy; later ones were usually hollow and cast in two pieces.

Neither buyer nor seller should consider breaking up a pair of candlesticks, as this lowers their value.

Left: Early pewter candlestick. Center: Hanging, wrought iron rush light also has socket for candle. Top right: Brass chamber stick has lever in shaft to push up candle stump. Bottom right: Early tin lantern used with candle.

OIL LAMPS Besides the almost bewildering diversity in the field of oil lamps, there is a two-fold interest for collectors: the style of the piece, and the method of combustion. **Betty** and **phoebe lamps** are oil lamps in their crudest form. Each has an oval-shaped fuel reservoir, either open or closed, and the wick emerges from the narrow end of the font. Sometimes

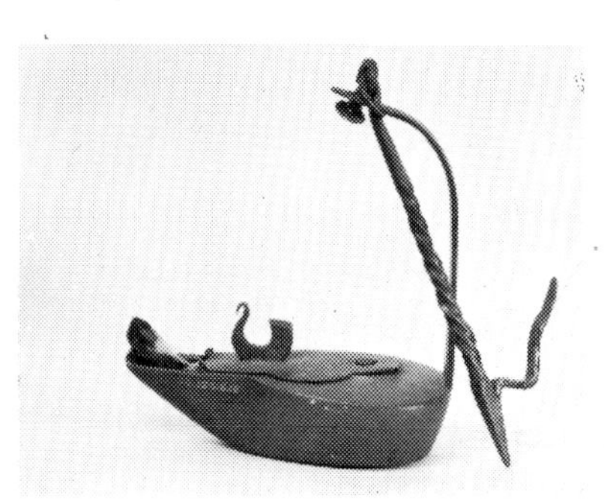

Top: Wrought iron betty lamp has hook for hanging. Bottom: Pair of early brass whale-oil lamps in simple candlestick shape, with double wicks. Right: Astral lamp has Argand burner with lusters and frosted glass shade.

a long hook for hanging it is part of the lamp itself. For fuel they burned oil or grease—animal, fish, or vegetable. The betty has a duct enclosing the upper portion of the wick; the phoebe, really a double betty, has, cupped beneath the fuel reservoir, a second vessel of the same shape to catch drippings. These lamps make picturesque accessories.

WHALE-OIL LAMPS Whale oil burned more cleanly than other fuels, and its availability in the late 1700's transformed lamp design. The earliest and simplest whale-oil lamps had closed reservoirs with one or two round wicks passing through the neck. Some were made like candlesticks with the font supported on a standard. Others, such as the bell-shaped lamps, were simply fonts that stood by themselves. Later lamps were quite complex.

Peg lamps were made by fitting a ball-shaped reservoir with a wick into the socket of a regular candlestick.

CAMPHENE LAMPS, c. 1830–50, look like whale-oil lamps, but have the wicks spread apart in a V shape to compensate for the extreme combustibility of the fuel, a mixture of alcohol and turpentine.

ARGAND LAMPS (**/***) The Argand whale-oil burner, the invention of a Swiss scientist, dominated lamp design between 1830 and 1850. A cylindrical burner with a tubular wick created an updraft of air at the center of the flame, causing it to burn brighter and cleaner. Many kinds of lamps used the Argand burner.

Astral lamps, usually ornate and columnar in design. A lamp of this Argand type has a ring-shaped reservoir that also serves as a rest for the shade.

Arm lamps have burner and shade on arm(s) projecting from standard that also supports fuel reservoir.

Mantel arm lamps, for parlor use, usually have two arms and the burners hung about with prisms (lusters).

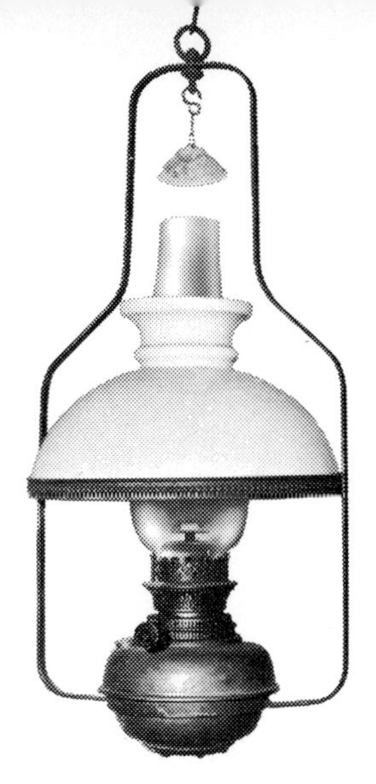

KEROSENE LAMPS were the preferred mode of lighting from 1865 to 1900. Fueled by a plentiful by-product of coal, they incorporated a reservoir, a dome-shaped flat-wick burner, and a chimney. The range of styles built around this basic design was typical of the period, from simple hand lamps to florid parlor pieces.

Rayo lamps are nickle-plated with glass umbrella shades.

"Gone with the Wind" lamps, c. 1880–1900, are made of glass or china and have a globular shade atop a matching globular reservoir.

Student lamps, of brass, single or double armed, have a lighting apparatus that can be moved up or down on a standard. A choice buy has the original shade.

Miniature lamps, no higher than nine inches, were once used as night lights. Especially prized now are those of art glass, pressed glass, or fine china. The gems of any collection, and the smallest, are the *nutmeg* lamps, in which the spice was once packaged for sale.

Hanging lamps are either the stationary type (out of stores, school, etc.), with glass or tin shades and simple

glass or brass fonts; or the movable type used in Victorian libraries and dining rooms, with pulleys, brass or iron frames hung with prisms, and painted glass or china shades.

ELECTRIFICATION Various fittings are available in hardware stores for adapting the burner sockets of oil lamps to electric light, and there are even small electric bulbs that give the effect of candlelight. Other antiques (bottles, guns, etc.) can be wired for light, though the job may require setting the object on a base. Wiring can be passed to the socket through pliable metal tubing; if left exposed, it should be of a color matching that of the piece.

PRICES for lamps vary widely. Here are some samples.

- * ($1–$25): betty lamps, glass hand-lamps
- ** ($25–$100): "Gone with the Wind" lamps, good miniature lamps, simple hanging lamps
- *** ($100–$250): electrified student lamps, lamps with Sandwich glass bases, decorative hall lamps, and hanging lamps

Types of kerosene lamps. Opposite page: Hanging lamp (left) is simple and functional in design; banquet lamp (right) has ornate porcelain globes. Above: Miniatures in glass and china include "Gone with the Wind" lamp at rear.

Collectors' Choice

Anything from a pittance to a small fortune can be spent in the following categories, each of which has a very special interest and appeal. Whichever one the collector chooses, he will find the competition for available items very keen indeed, and communication among enthusiasts extraordinarily lively.

Dolls

The doll world has much of the diversity and fascination of the real world it imitates, with almost limitless variations in the age, materials, construction, personality, and dress of dolls. And, though prices for them run high, antique dolls are in wide demand.

WOODEN DOLLS Of the simple wooden dolls that have delighted children for centuries, perhaps none has been more widely enjoyed than the type known in England as **Flanders babies** and in America as **penny woodens.** These peg-jointed dolls stand from 3½ to 9 inches high and have sketchily painted features (*/**).

Some wooden dolls were dressed elaborately. England's **Pedlar dolls,** modeled after the "notion nannys" who went about London on foot, were dressed in voluminous skirts and laden down with tiny wares—pots, cutlery, laces, stockings, and the like (**). The **Queen Anne dolls** of the 1700's, exquisitely costumed and their cheeks highly colored, had great favor (**/***).

In America, a fully-articulated doll with slot and tenon joints was manufactured in 1873 by **Joel Ellis** of Springfield, Vt. These rock maple figures had hands and feet of pewter or iron and measured 12 to 18 inches

Chapter opening: French Jumeau doll. Below, from left: Wooden doll with plaster-covered head; Joel Ellis jointed wooden doll; group of china-headed dolls; composition doll with glass eyes.

high. Production lasted only a year, but closely similar dolls were made later by other manufacturers using joints of stronger construction. Ellis-type dolls, c. 1873–82, are very rare finds today (***).

Another outstanding American-made doll, the **Schoenhut,** with spring-hinge joints, was patented about 1911. Baby and child figures were made in sizes from 11 to 21 inches; heads were modeled in basswood and later ones had hair wigs attached (**). Albert Schoenhut also made delightful circus animal figures (*).

CHINA AND CHINA-HEADED DOLLS (**) are noted for their individuality. Almost all china centers made dolls, in Germany especially, and much of the work involved was done by hand. Added variety was provided by the vogue for "character dolls" such as "Jenny Lind" and "Queen Victoria." Most china dolls have molded hair, usually glossy black. Deep shoulders and a thin red line above the eye to suggest an eyelid are marks of early vintage in china dolls, while high-heeled shoes did not appear until 1860. Many china heads are marked on the inside.

BISQUE AND PARIAN DOLLS (of unglazed china) are grouped separately from china dolls. Fine bisques

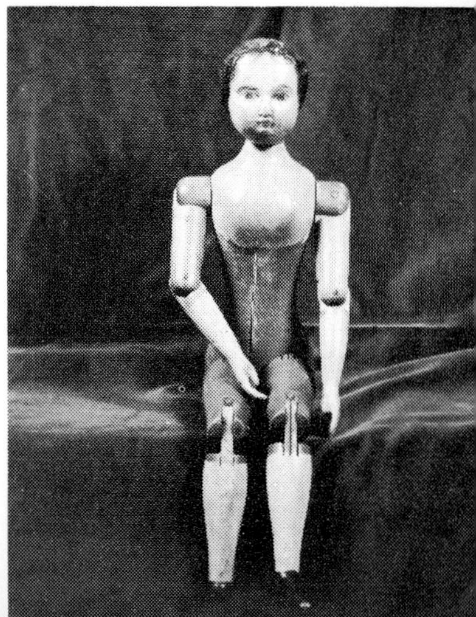

come from France and Germany. Some American makers experimented with them but the quality was not equal to the imports. Parian heads were untinted but bisques were usually delicately tinted, at least after 1850 (**/***).

Frozen Charlottes (*/**) are small, rigid dolls of glazed china or bisque, popularized by German makers between 1865–70, and favorites with today's collectors.

Jumeau dolls (***), with faces dominated by large, lovely eyes, are the best-loved of the French bisques. Early ones had stationary, blown-glass eyes and closed mouths. In the 1860's the dolls were given swivel heads, and about 1880 baby and child Jumeaus were made in addition to the slim-waisted lady dolls of earlier years. Real hair is a feature of the later Jumeaus. Trade marking of the dolls began only in 1880.

Bru dolls (***), rivals of the early Jumeaus, are in somewhat heavier proportion, though quite charming. Most are marked.

Later German bisques—by Steiner (***), Simon & Halbig, Kestner, Reinhardt and many others—are being eagerly collected and generally sell for less (**). Collectors in this field will need a book of doll marks.

PAPIER MÂCHÉ and COMPOSITION (sawdust

with a glue binder) were extensively used by both European and American doll manufacturers in the 1800's.

In 1858 **Ludwig Greiner** of Philadelphia patented "improved" papier mâché heads to which buyers attached homemade bodies. There were several boy and girl styles, all with molded hair. Interior and seams were reinforced with stiffened fabric, a feature later copied by other manufacturers. It's hard to identify a Greiner positively unless it carries a label, as most did, on a spot between the shoulder blades. Though Greiners are no longer plentiful, Greiner-type and later composition dolls are easy to find (**).

WAX DOLLS of the early 1800's had head and shoulders of either solid or hollow-molded wax, attached to bodies of wood, cloth, or kid. Later, stronger dolls were made with a molded base of papier mâché or composition, which was usually painted with the features before receiving the surface coating of hot wax.

Montanari dolls (***) were baby dolls with heads made surprisingly lifelike by a process of embedding individual hairs in the wax with a hot needle. Other makers, notably Marsh and Pierotti, also used this process in

making dolls of distinction. If one of these rare and beautiful productions of the 1850's can be found today, it is probably worth whatever price is asked.

Still available are many of the mass-produced wax dolls of the early 1900's, with less delicately modeled features and bodies of straw-stuffed muslin (**).

The age of wax dolls is hard to place, as few were marked. Here again, experts make deductions from points of styling, such as the molded bonnets of the 1860's and the period of the clothes if the original ones are still intact.

FABRIC DOLLS (**/***) include both homemade rag dolls and the more sophisticated fabric dolls made by professionals. Standouts among U.S.-made dolls are those of the late 1800's by **Mrs. Izannah Walker** (R.I.) with features in raised and painted relief, and the **Martha Chase Stockinette dolls** that first appeared commercially in 1897. From Europe we have the artistic felt dolls of **Madame Lenci** (Italy), the sturdy and appealing child dolls of **Frau Kathe Kruse** (Germany), and the highly individualized figures made in France (and later in the U.S.) by **Bernard Ravaca.**

VALUE in dolls depends to some extent on rarity and dress. Clothes should be original. If not, they should be authentic in period and material.

CARE of dolls calls for an atmosphere free of moths and dust, well humidified and moderate in temperature (last point very important for wax dolls). Clothes must be washed or cleaned with great care. Serious repair should be done by doll hospitals (found all over the country). For display set dolls, supported on metal stands, in a cabinet with glass doors. (See antiques magazines for addresses of doll supply firms.) Dolls not on display can be stored in plastic bags.

Left: Montanari doll in heirloom christening garb has real hair, lifelike appearance. Next to it, an open-mouthed Bru doll of unglazed china, also with real hair. Right: Appealing homemade rag doll.

Top: Appealing lamb is squeak toy of mid-1800's. Its coat is natural lamb's wool, wooden legs are hand carved. Above: Ives toy locomotive and coal tender, vintage 1904.

Toys

Toys are delightful collectors' items. Their appeal varies from the gaiety of tin and iron toys to the amusing ingenuity of mechanical banks. While many toys are inexpensive, some are very expensive, depending upon rarity, design, workmanship, and condition—preferably original, neither reconstructed nor refinished. Dates are not of primary importance to the toy collector; some, in fact, want only commercially made pieces of as recent date as the early 1900's. Unmarked toys of the 19th century can sometimes be identified from the catalogues of toy manufacturers and mail-order houses. These old catalogues sell at antiques sales (*) and are themselves worthy of collecting.

The earliest American toys, found today only in museums, were homemade, often whittled from wood. As the country developed, toy making was taken up by tinsmiths, potters, pewterers, and glassmakers. Around the mid-1700's, toy shops appeared in New England and Pennsylvania. After 1830, industrialization brought toy making to the status of big business, built on novelty, quality, and quantity.

TIN TOYS (*/**) made in quantity c. 1840–1900, include gaily-painted or lithographed dolls' dishes and furniture, animals, boats, trains, and horse-drawn vehicles, many operated by clockwork. Available.

IRON TOYS (**) c. 1880–1912, were generally "transportation toys" of painted cast iron. Most are of the pull type; a few are mechanized. Farm equipment, circus wagons, fire engines, carriages, tallyhos, and trains can be found. **Bell Toys,** when pushed or pulled, animate a figure which rings a bell. Available.

TRAINS (**) range from early wooden ones, to windup tin trains (1870), rare steam-run engines (1870–80), and, after 1900, electric trains. Joshua Lionel Cowan's first

model train, the battery-operated Lionel, appeared about 1903; the first electric Lionel train in 1906. Lionel trains of up to 1930 vintage, and the early trains made by Ives of Bridgeport are among the most valuable. Prices depend on how much of the set is original. Besides the cars, collectors also look for miniature watertowers, signals, stations, etc. All are available.

CAP PISTOLS (*/**) of the late 1800's to early 1900's are especially delightful for the animation that occurs when the trigger is pulled. The human and animal figures that move (monkey, Punch and Judy, etc.) are part of the pistol's design. Patent date and occasionally maker's name are impressed on the barrel. **Clapper heads,** which explode when dropped, are also in this category. All are available.

MECHANICAL BANKS (**/****) c. 1870–1910, distinctively American pieces which animate when a penny

is deposited, were made of cast iron or sometimes of tin, and were painted in bright colors. Here again, catalogues can help in identifying the more than 250 named pieces. Rarest and most expensive (over $3,000) is the "Harlequin, Clown, and Columbine" bank, whose figures revolve in a dance. Value lies in authenticity, scarcity, and condition. Available.

MARBLES (*) were introduced into the colonies by the Dutch. Taws (shooters), cut from marble, cobalt, onyx, jasper, or jade, were imported from Europe throughout the 18th and 19th centuries. In the early 1900's (until World War I), marbles were imported chiefly from Germany. As for domestic production, "aggies" were made in Ohio as early as the 1890's, but it was not until the invention of a marble-making machine in 1915 that U.S. industry expanded to fill the demand. All types are available.

Opposite page: In clown cap pistol (top), mule kicks when trigger is pulled; animated savings bank (left & right) has whirling clown. Above: Group of toys includes tin tallyho pull toy, Schoenhut circus figures, and glass marbles.

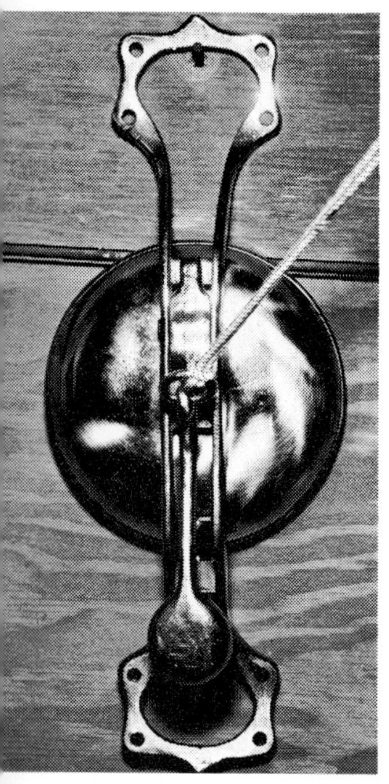

Top: Brass sleigh bells of the type belted to harness under horse's chin. Bottom left: Old trolley bell that converts easily for use as doorbell. Bottom right: Hand bells probably made for use in church.

Bells

Bells in early colonial days were usually made of iron. Improvement came in the mid-1700's, when a bronze "bell metal," combining three or four parts of copper to one of tin, became available.

Handbells (*) of brass or bell metal had turned wooden handles. The largest, once used by town criers, measure 15 inches high. The smallest, standing 5 inches, were used in school rooms to call for order. Available.

Sleigh bells (*/**) date to the early 1800's. Brass bells are superior in tone and craftsmanship to iron ones. The choice buys are bells still attached to their original, unbroken leather. They are attached with staples or cotter pins and can be easily removed for cleaning. A full string may include thirty or more in matching or graduated sizes from one inch to 2½ inches. Parts of strings are often used as doorbells.

A string should cost about $1.00 to $1.50 per bell, unless they are burnished or exceptional for some other feature. Available.

Horse bells (**) of brass were mounted on a strip of metal and attached to the hame (collar) of a draft horse. Finest and best-known are the Conestoga bells, in sets of three, four, and five, used on the horses that drew the Conestoga wagons west. Horse bells are available though not common.

Other fine bells available at reasonable prices are store, farm, altar, fire-engine, trolley, and ship bells. Also, there are the push-button call bells used to summon help in old-time stores and offices, and antique doorbells of the type sounded by pulling a chain.

Glass and ceramic bells (**) are of special interest for the glass or china of which they are made. Bells of Nailsea, cranberry glass, cut glass, and Venetian latticino are prized.

Buttons

Buttons are popular with collectors because of their attractiveness, historic interest, convenient size for storage and display, and wide price range (from less than $1.00 to as much as $100 for a single button). Used for centuries, not only as fasteners on clothing but as decorative trim and symbols of rank, buttons can be found in great variety and may be classified under several headings.

AGE: Ornamental buttons were known in ancient Egypt. As fasteners they have existed in Europe since the Dark Ages. These would be museum pieces, however. Most collectibles date from the 18th and 19th centuries.

MATERIALS: China, glass, metal, wood, ivory, composition, bone, fabric, shell, plastic, leather, rubber, papier mâché, and precious and semi-precious stones.

CONSTRUCTION: With various kinds of shanks and

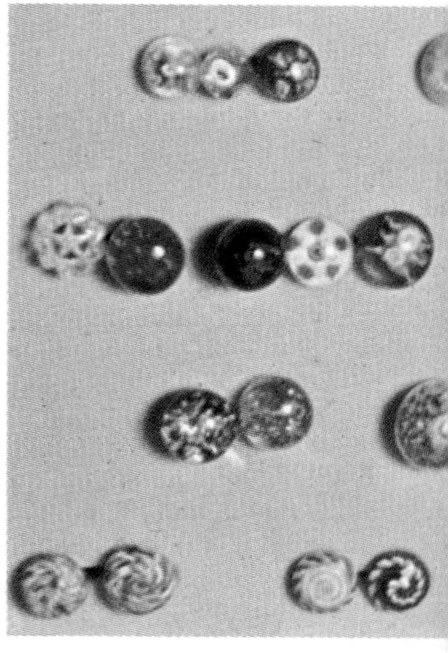

Left: Button collection, including cameos and painted miniatures, has heads as theme. Center: "Paperweight" buttons in millefiore, candy swirl, and other patterns. Right: Well-arranged collection of Civil War uniform buttons.

sew-through holes, with or without facings, backs, etc.
COUNTRY OF ORIGIN: Buttons are collected from all parts of the world. France, England, and 19th-century America are excellent sources of fine and fancy ones.
DESIGN: Quaint and attractive—expensive, too—are ships, locomotives, balloons, and portraits. Historic buttons, such as those made in celebration of Lafayette's visit to America, are also sought. Men collectors favor colonials (17th and 18th century buttons, usually of brass that has been hand-chased or machine-turned), and military, uniform, or campaign buttons.

Most collectors mount buttons on 9x12 cards, which may then be either framed or stored flat.

Local button collectors' clubs, especially those affiliated with the National Button Society, make available the latest button news, and facilitate the buying, selling, and exchanging of buttons among collectors.

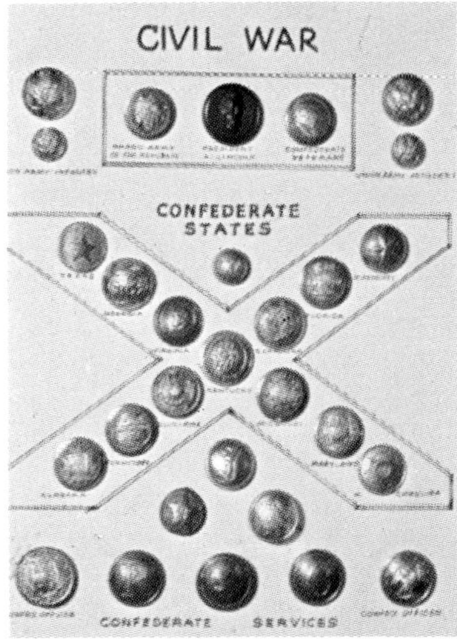

Ephemera

Ephemera (from the Greek, meaning "short-lived") is the term used for collectible paper items: old greeting cards, documents, programs, maps, posters, newspapers, etc. Collectors who choose this field will find a wide variety of inexpensive and easily stored items available.

GREETING CARDS (*) come in several varieties, of which **valentines** are the oldest. Earliest American valentines, dating to about 1750, were painted, pin-pricked, folded, or cut out, all by hand. The sentiments could be original or chosen ready-made from a book called a "writer." England produced commercial valentines, printed and lithographed, around 1840. About ten years later, commercial production was initiated in America by Esther Howland, a Massachusetts girl. Her cards, signed with an "H" in a red heart, were the best in the commercial field for many years and are prized by collectors today. The fussy valentines of the late Victorian era are less desirable than earlier cards, but anything earlier than 1890 has some value.

Christmas cards were produced in England in limited quantity as early as 1840. They were made in the U.S. by Esther Howland in the 1860's, by Louis Prang, the Boston lithographer, in 1874, and were in general use a few years later. Easter cards followed soon after.

Scrapbooks (*), a fad of the later 1800's, were used to preserve all kinds of paper items too pretty to throw away: greeting cards, lithographs, trade cards (advertisements), and the like. Scrapbooks are available and are not usually broken up for sale.

In days when color printing was still a novelty, collectors filled scrapbooks with eye-catching items like those at top. Bottom: Expandable paper valentine of 1880's is example of Victorian style in greeting cards.

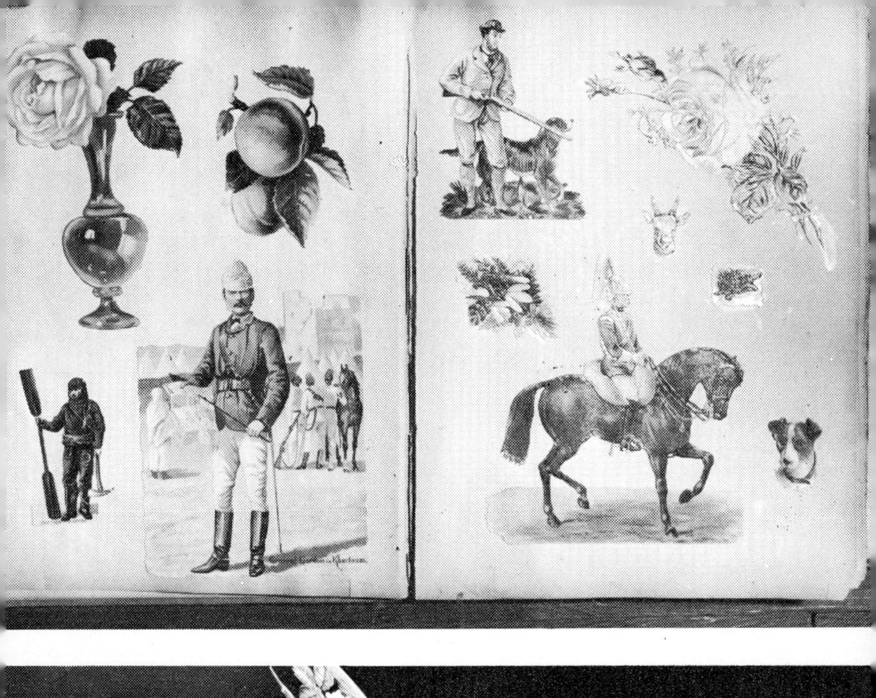

Paper dolls (*) were first made commercially in America around 1854, many—including the famous Tom Thumb and family—by McLoughlin Brothers of New York. The earliest cutouts were printed by *Godey's Lady's Book* in 1859. In the 1890's paper dolls were used as giveaways to advertise soap, coffee, and thread. Certain series, such as English Queens, and ballet and military dolls, are more valuable than others. The real prizes in this field are homemade dolls of the pre-commercial period, cut from tissue or fancy paper. Paper dolls are available, though not common.

Other paper items being collected are almanacs, catalogues, playing cards, post cards, old music and song books, drawing books, account books, needlework patterns, time tables, handbills, and political fliers.

These paper items should be exposed to the air as little as possible. Fine pieces can be framed for display and the rest of a collection kept in envelopes or loose-leaf display pages made of clear plastic. All are available.

Nineteenth-century paper dolls include "A Little Girl's Doll," English boxed set with eight different dresses and hats, and "The History of Little Fanny," an English storybook doll of 1811.

Bibliography

It is characteristic of collectors to want to share the joy and challenge of their avocation. And so this book has been written, both to provide basic information about American antiques and to stimulate the reader's interest in them. Full enjoyment of antiques comes from truly knowing them, and it is hoped that the following list of books will help collectors on their way to erudition in the fields of their choice.

General Information

THE CONCISE ENCYCLOPEDIA OF AMERICAN ANTIQUES, *2 vols., Helen Comstock, ed., Hawthorn Books*

THE EASY EXPERT IN COLLECTING AND RESTORING AMERICAN ANTIQUES, *Moreton Marsh, J. B. Lippincott Co.*

A HANDBOOK OF AMERICAN ANTIQUES, *Katherine Morrison McClinton, Random House*

HANDMADE IN AMERICA, *Sigmund A. Lavine, Dodd, Mead & Co.*

HOW TO KNOW AMERICAN ANTIQUES, *Alice Winchester, Dodd, Mead & Co.*

VICTORIAN ANTIQUES, *Thelma Shull, Charles E. Tuttle Co.*

Furniture

AMERICAN COUNTRY FURNITURE, 1780–1875, *Ralph & Terry Kovel, Crown Pubs.*

AMERICAN FURNITURE, *Helen Comstock, Viking*

FIELD GUIDE TO EARLY AMERICAN FURNITURE *and* FIELD GUIDE TO AMERICAN VICTORIAN FURNITURE, *Thomas H. Ormsbee, Little, Brown and Co.*

FURNITURE TREASURY, *Wallace Nutting, Macmillan*

HANDBOOK OF ANTIQUE CHAIRS, *Carl Drepperd, Doubleday*

Glass

AMERICAN GLASS, *Helen & George S. McKearing, Crown Pubs.*

AMERICAN CUT AND ENGRAVED GLASS *and* AMERICAN PRESSED GLASS AND FIGURE BOTTLES, *Albert C. Revi, Thomas Nelson & Sons*

BITTERS BOTTLES, *Richard Watson, Thomas Nelson & Sons*

EARLY AMERICAN PRESSED GLASS, *Ruth Webb Lee, Lee Publications*

MILK GLASS, *Eugene M. Belknap, Crown Pubs.*

OLD GLASS PAPERWEIGHTS, *Evangeline Bergstrom, Crown Pubs.*

NINETEENTH CENTURY GLASS, *Albert C. Revi, Thomas Nelson & Sons*

China

EARLY AMERICAN POTTERY AND CHINA, *John Spargo, Garden City Publishing Co.*

HANDBOOK OF OLD POTTERY AND PORCELAIN MARKS, *C. Jordan Thorn, Tudor Publishing Co.*

VICTORIAN POTTERY AND PORCELAIN, *G. Bernard Hughes, Country Life Ltd., London*

Metals

AMERICAN SILVER, *Millicent Stow, M. Barrows & Co.*

ANTIQUE TIN & TOLEWARE, *Mary Earle Guild, Charles E. Tuttle Co.*

THE BOOK OF OLD SILVER, *Seymour B. Wyler, Crown Pubs.*

A DIRECTORY OF AMERICAN SILVER, PEWTER, AND SILVER PLATE, *Ralph & Terry Kovel, Crown Pubs.*

EARLY AMERICAN COPPER, TIN, AND BRASS, *Henry J. Kaufmann, McBride Co.*

EARLY AMERICAN WROUGHT IRON, *Albert M. Sonn, Scribner's*

GUIDE TO AMERICAN PEWTER, *Carl Jacobs, McBride Co.*

SOUVENIR SPOONS OF THE '90's, *Anton Hardt, New York*

Primitives

EARLY AMERICAN WOODEN WARE, *Mary Earle Guild, Charles E. Tuttle Co.*

FOLK ART OF RURAL PENNSYLVANIA, *Frances M. Lichten, Scribner's*

PICTORIAL FOLK ART, *Alice Ford, Studio Publications*

Lighting

COLONIAL LIGHTING, *Arthur M. Hayward, Little, Brown & Co.*

FLICKERING FLAMES, *Leroy L. Thwing, Charles E. Tuttle Co.*

Clocks

AMERICAN CLOCKS AND CLOCKMAKERS, *Carl W. Drepperd, Charles T. Branford (pub.)*

THE BOOK OF AMERICAN CLOCKS, *Brooks Palmer, Macmillan*

Other Collectibles

BUTTON CLASSICS, *Laura Erwinna Crouse & Marguerite Maple, Lightner Publishing Co.*

A HISTORY OF VALENTINES, *Ruth Webb Lee, Lee Publications*

MECHANICAL TOY BANKS, *Louis H. Hertz, Mark Haber & Co.*

OLD DOLLS, *Eleanor St. George, M. Barrows & Co.*

TOYS IN AMERICA, *Marshall & Inez McClintock, Public Affairs Press*

Index